I0468712

Adult Coloring Book

Relaxing Mandala Designs Stress Relieving Patterns

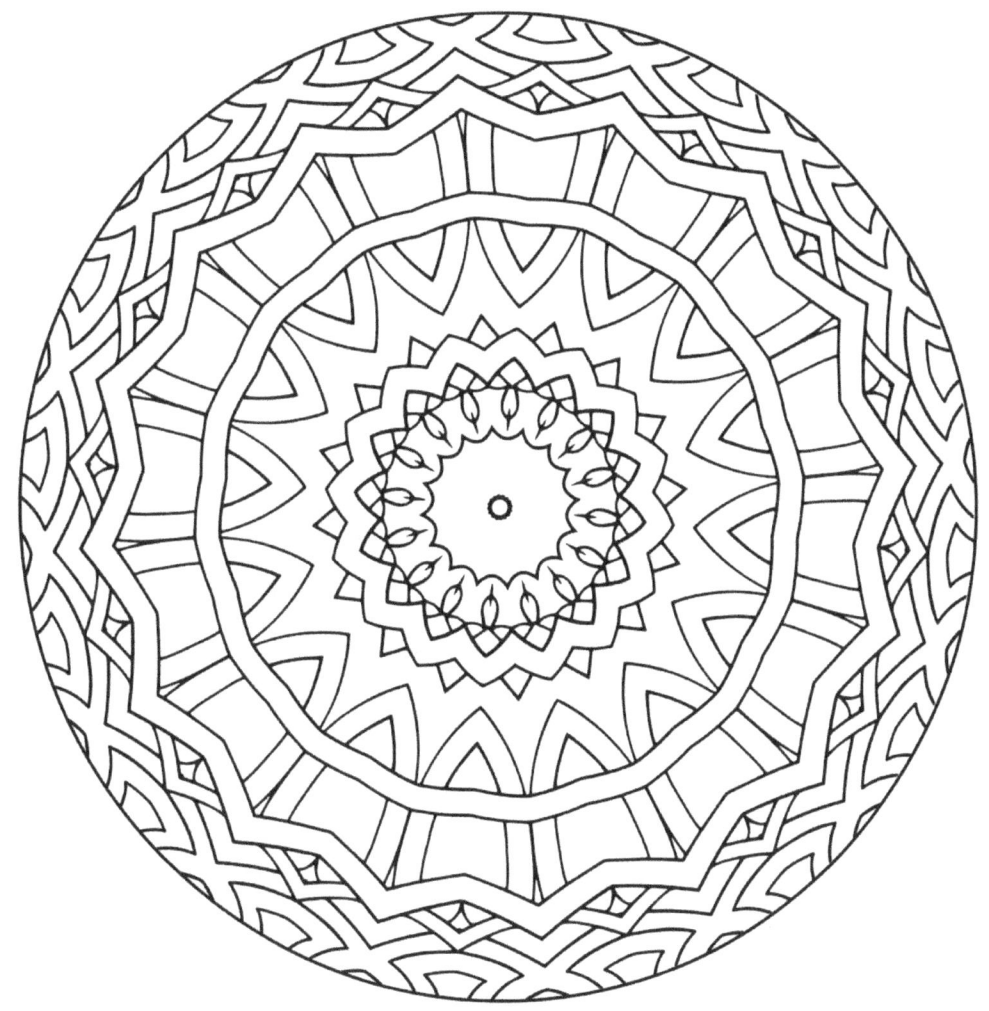

Created by KM Writing Incorporated

Art is an international language understood by all. ~Igor Babailov

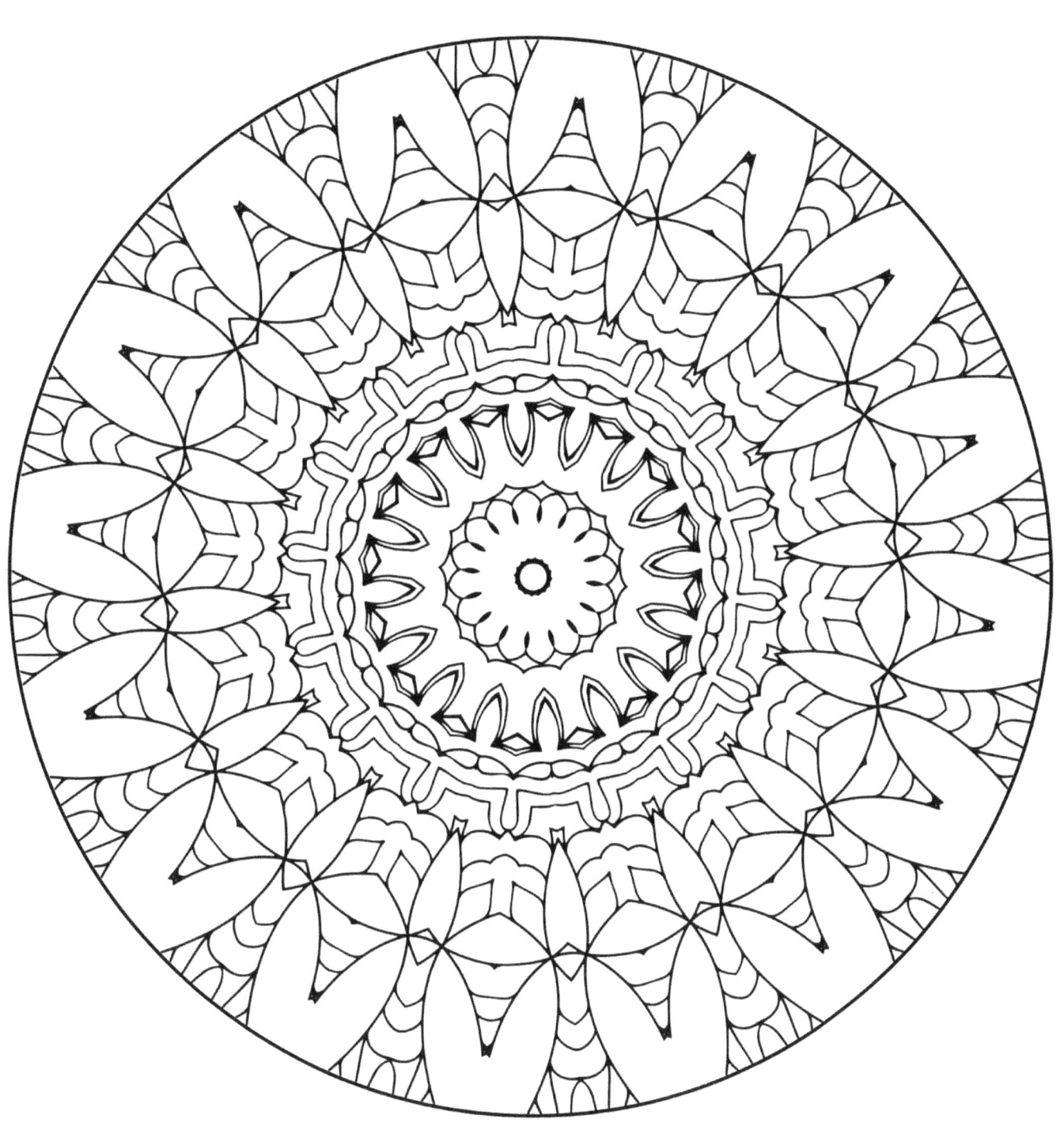

Art enables us to find ourselves and lose ourselves at the same time.
~ Thomas Merton

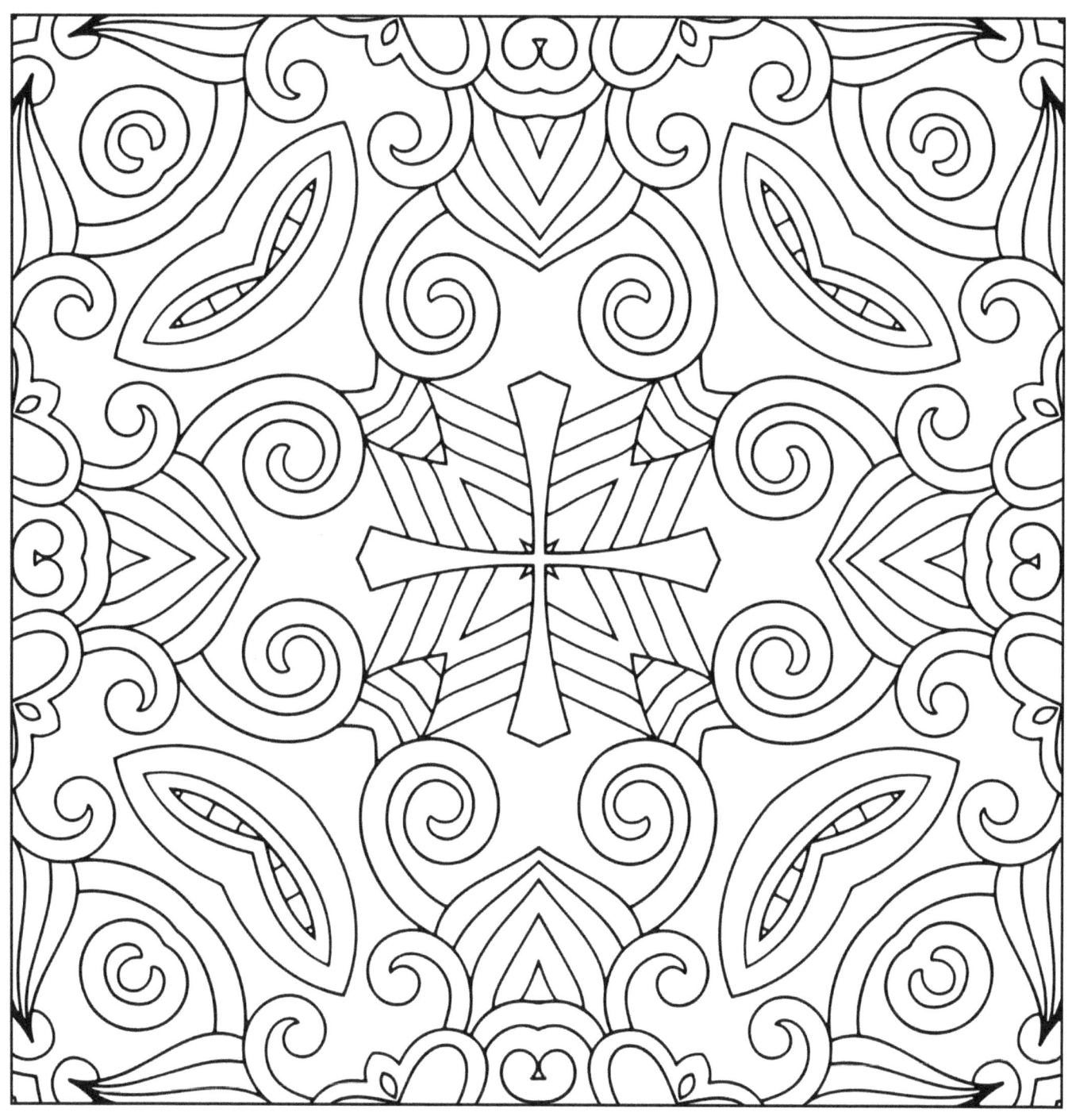

Choose joy, give freely and love always.

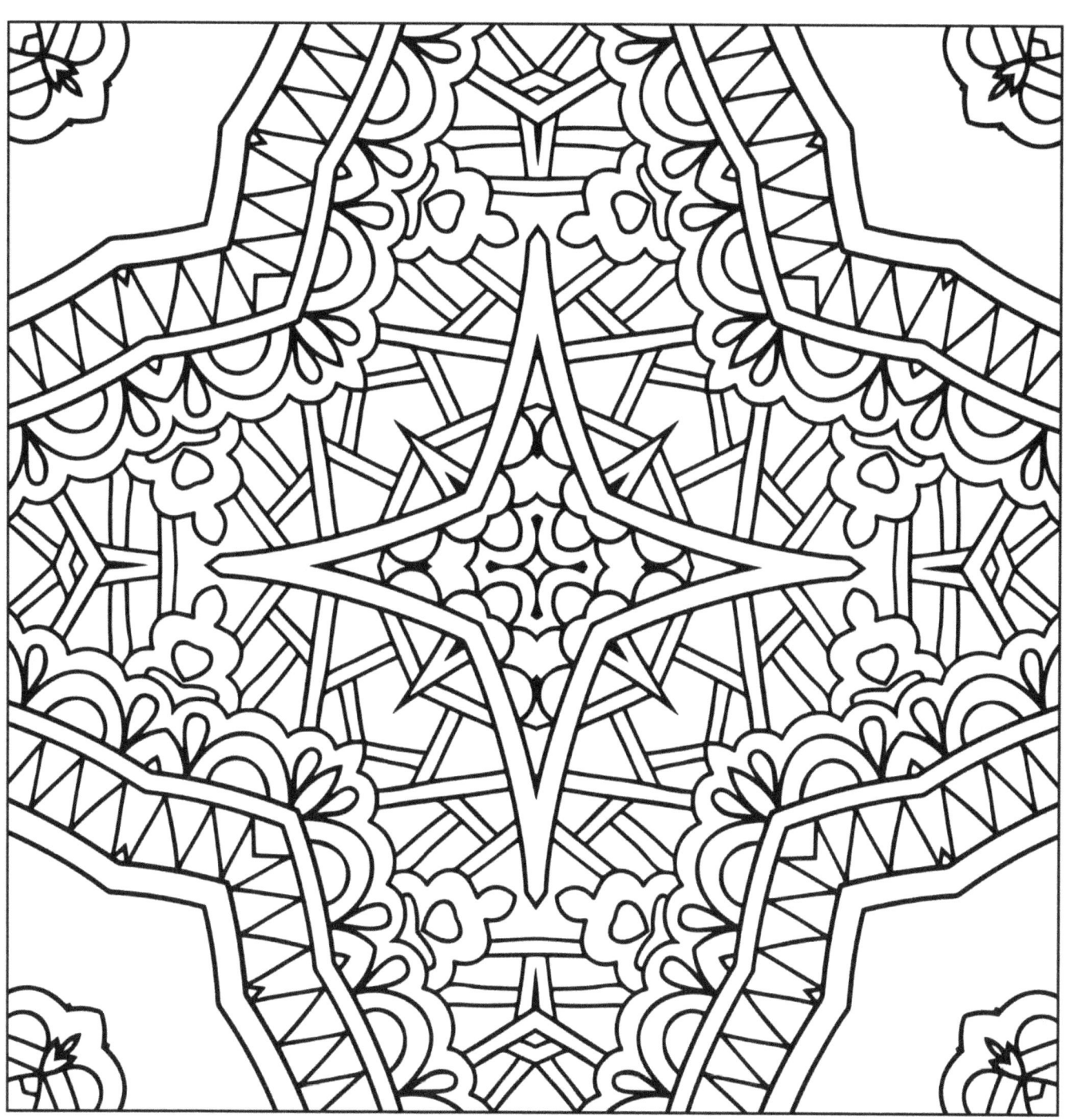

Sometimes the smallest things take
up the most room in your heart.
~ Winnie the Pooh

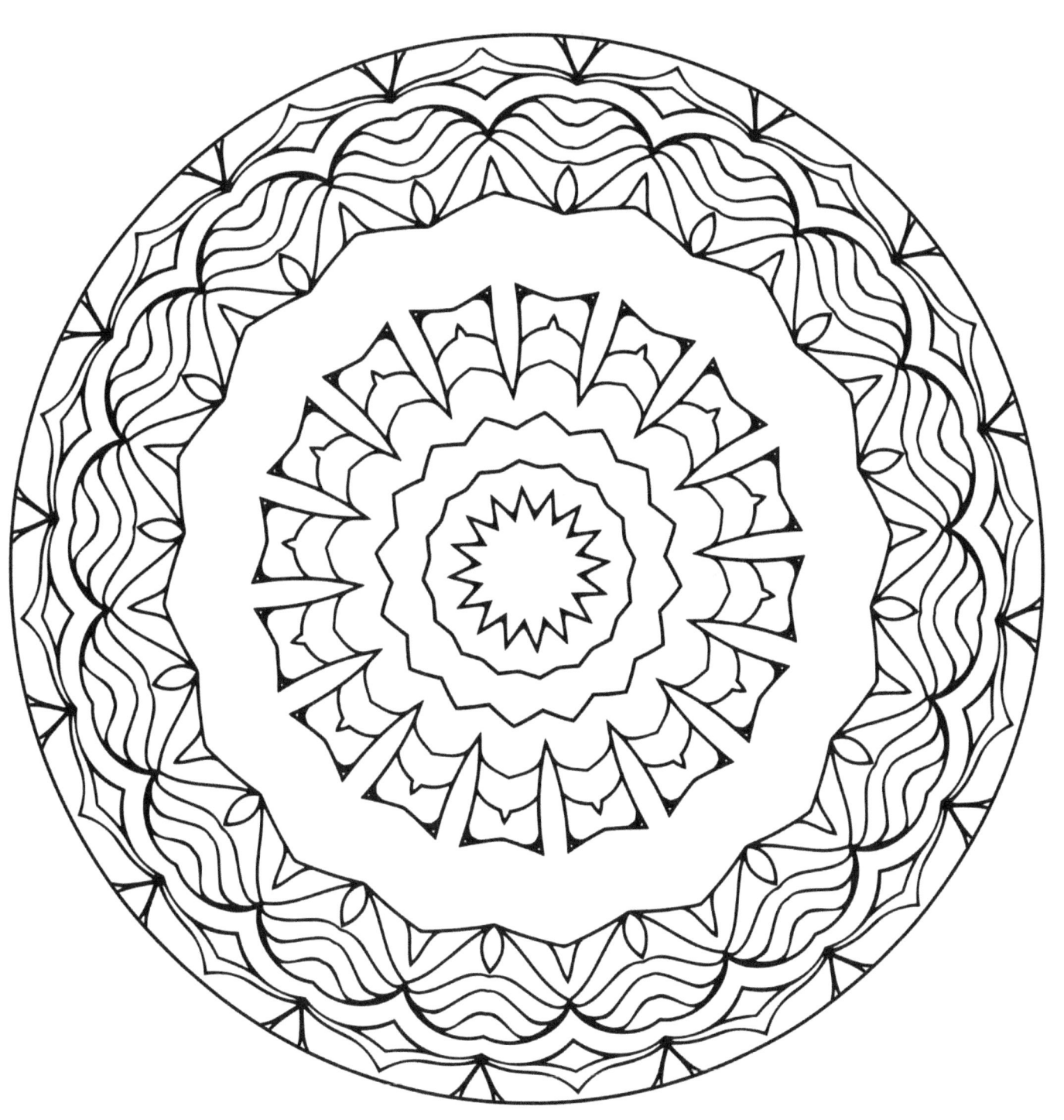

Start by doing what's necessary; then do what's possible; and suddenly you are doing the impossible.

~ Saint Francis of Assisi

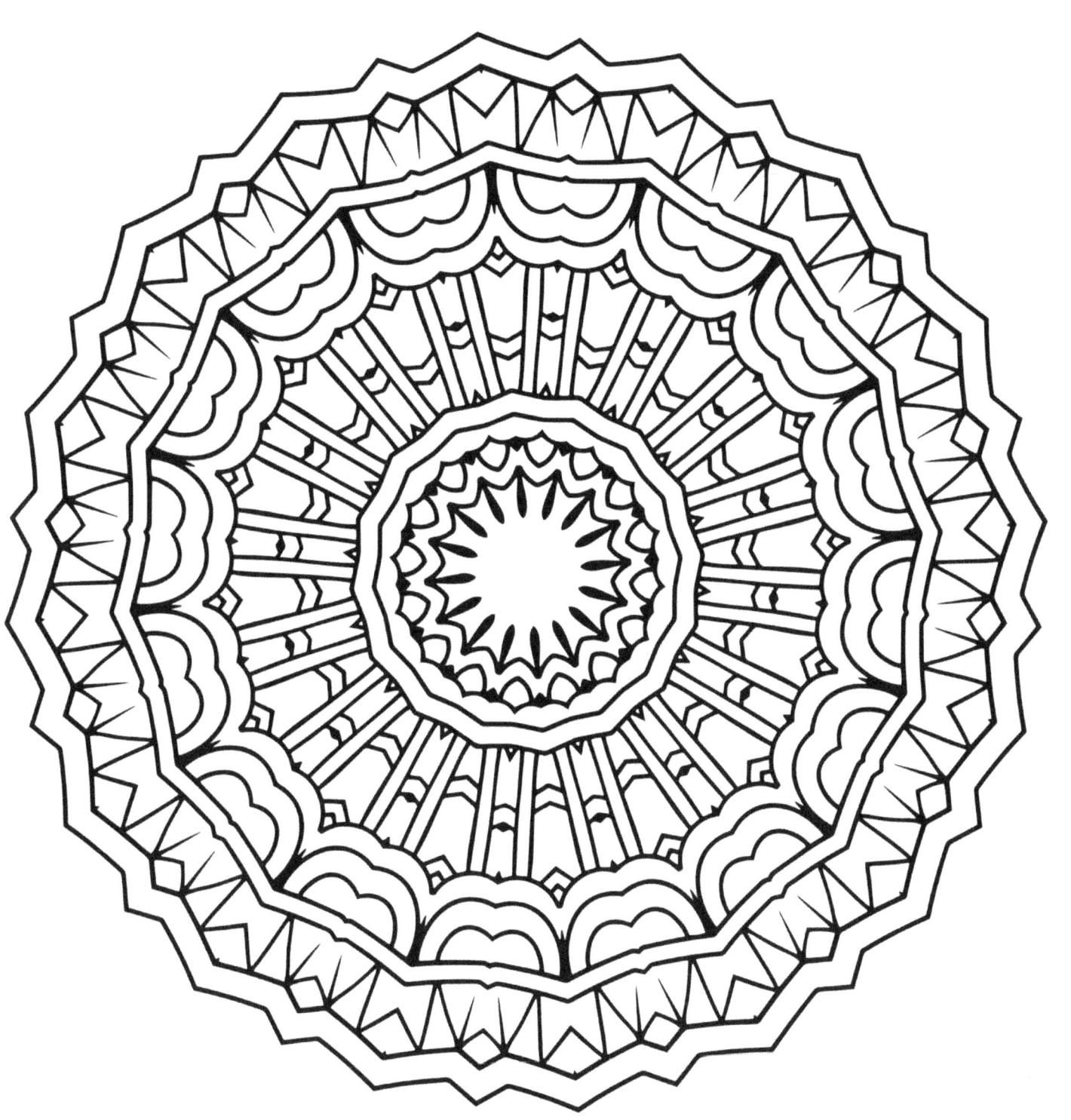

Let know man pull you low enough to hate him. ~ Martin Luther King Jr.

We do not remember days, we
remember moments.

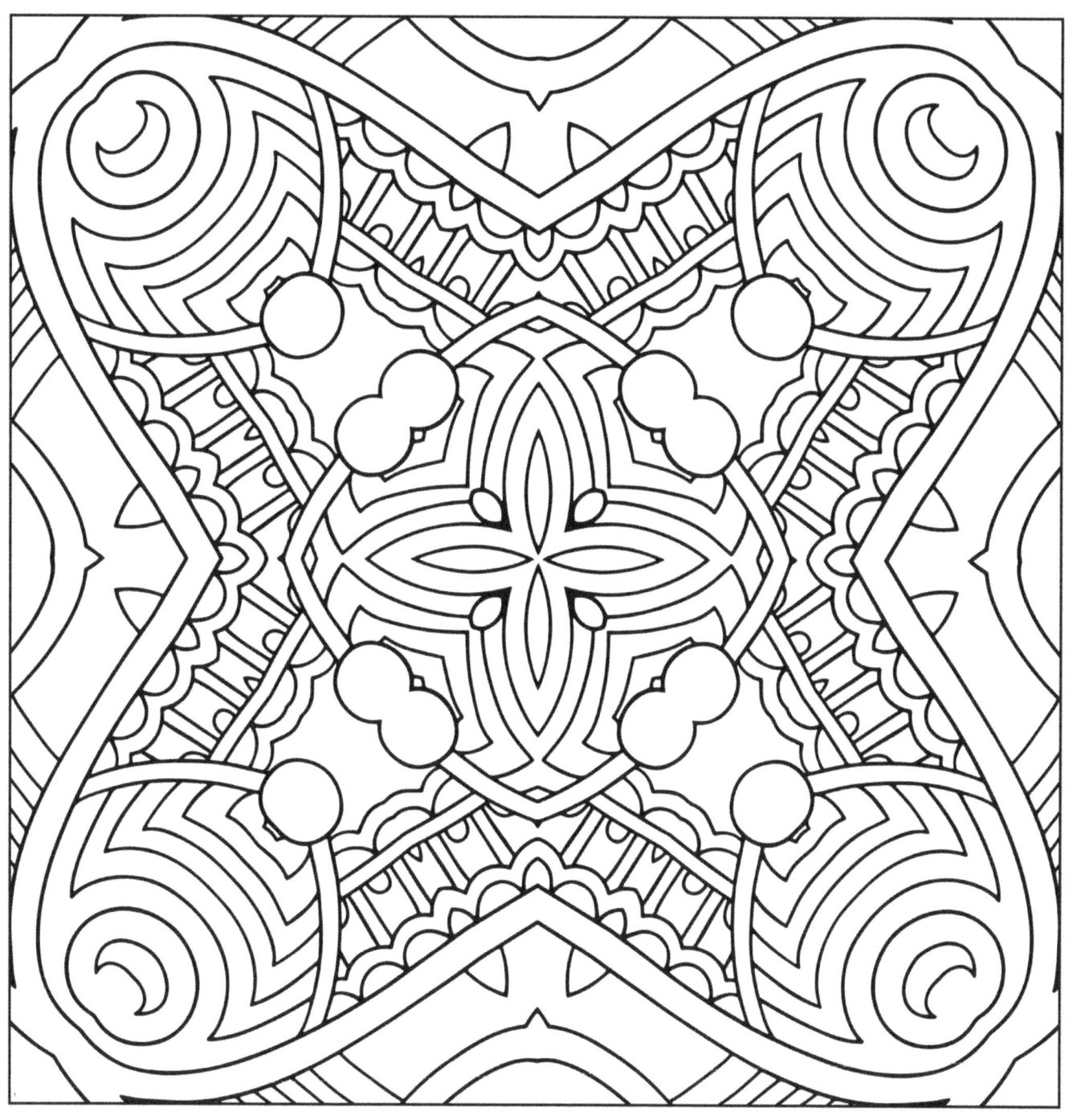

It's the possibility of having a dream

come true that makes life

interesting.

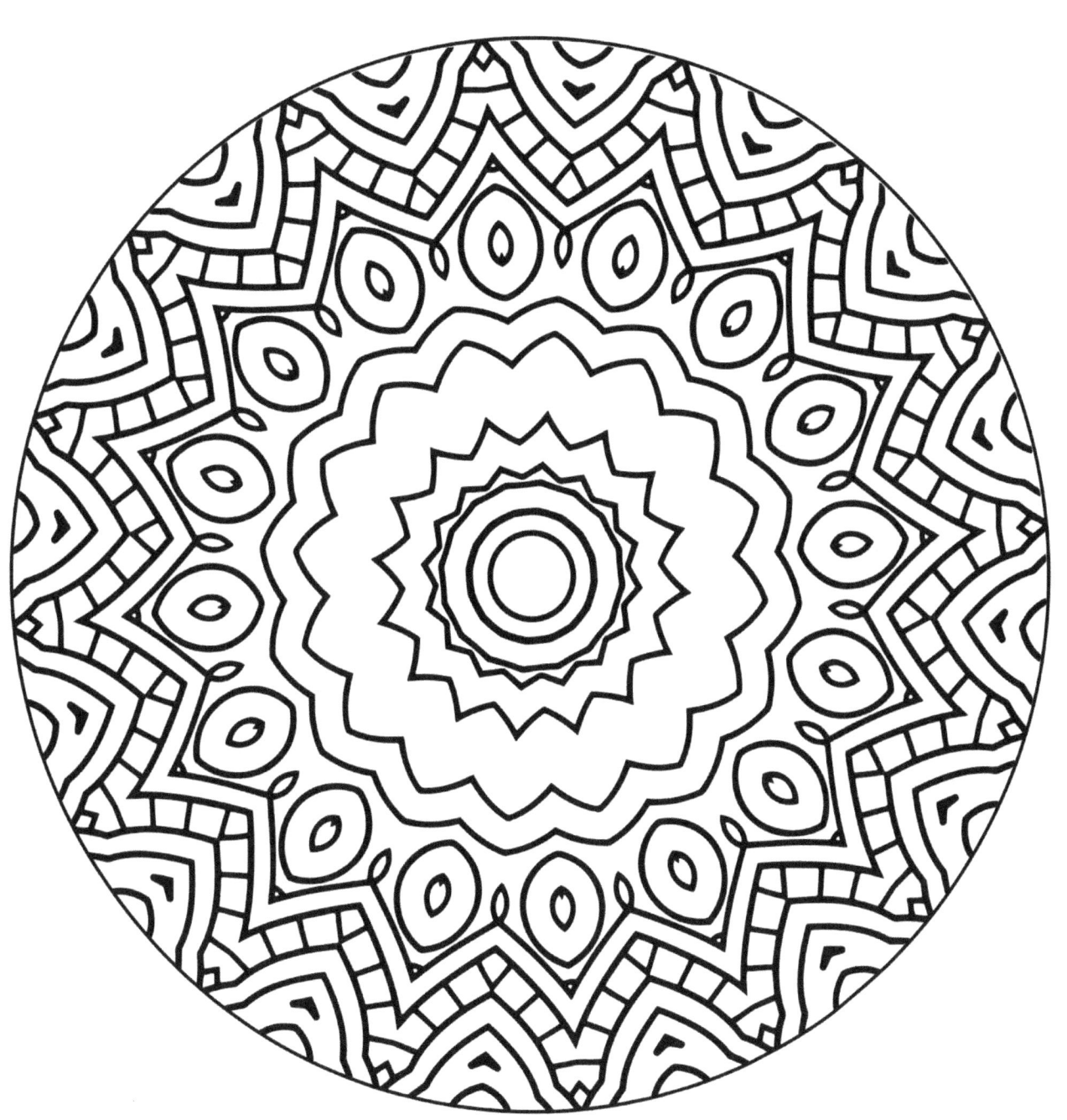

I'm lost; lost in my day dreams.

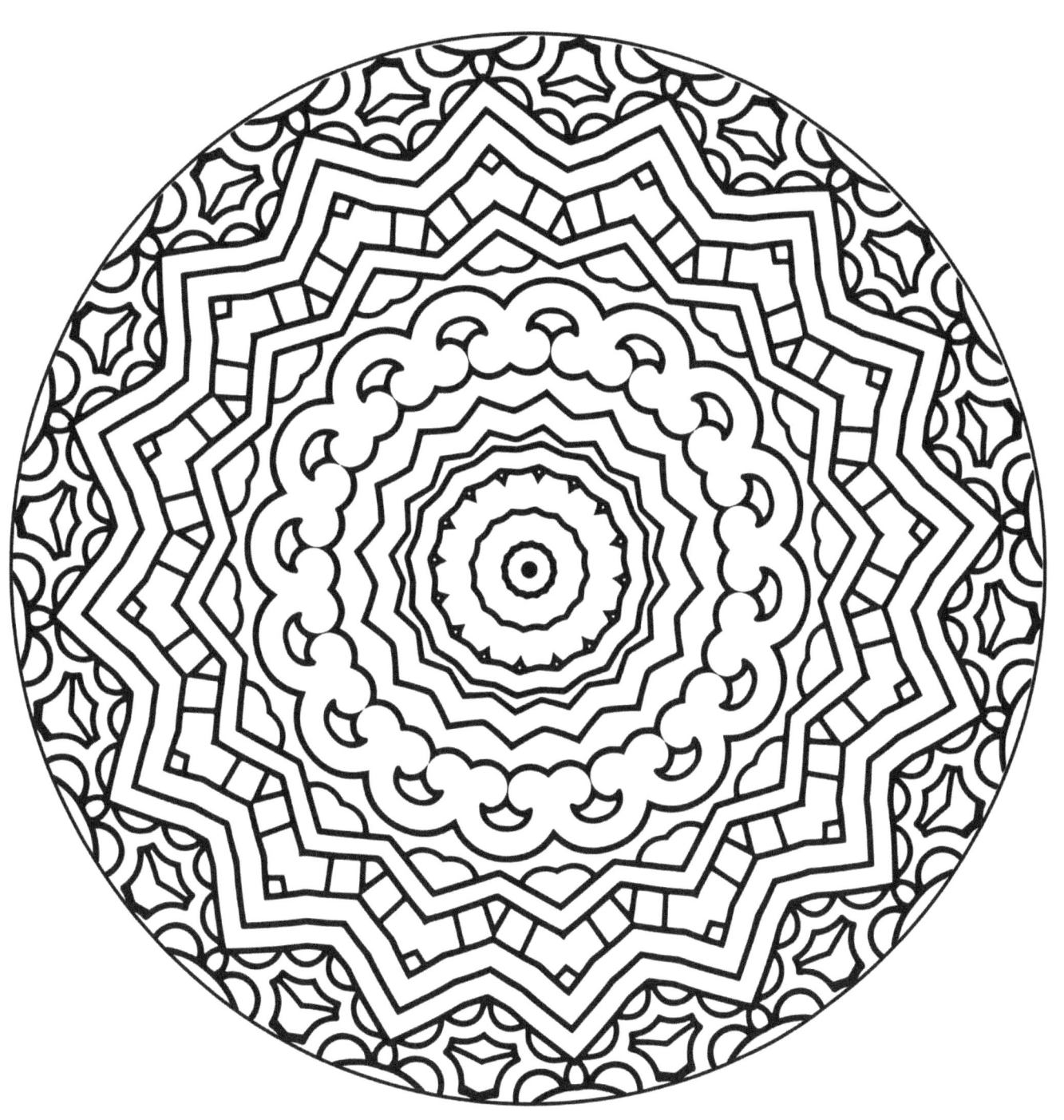

As soon as I saw you, I knew an adventure was going to happen.
~ Winnie the Pooh

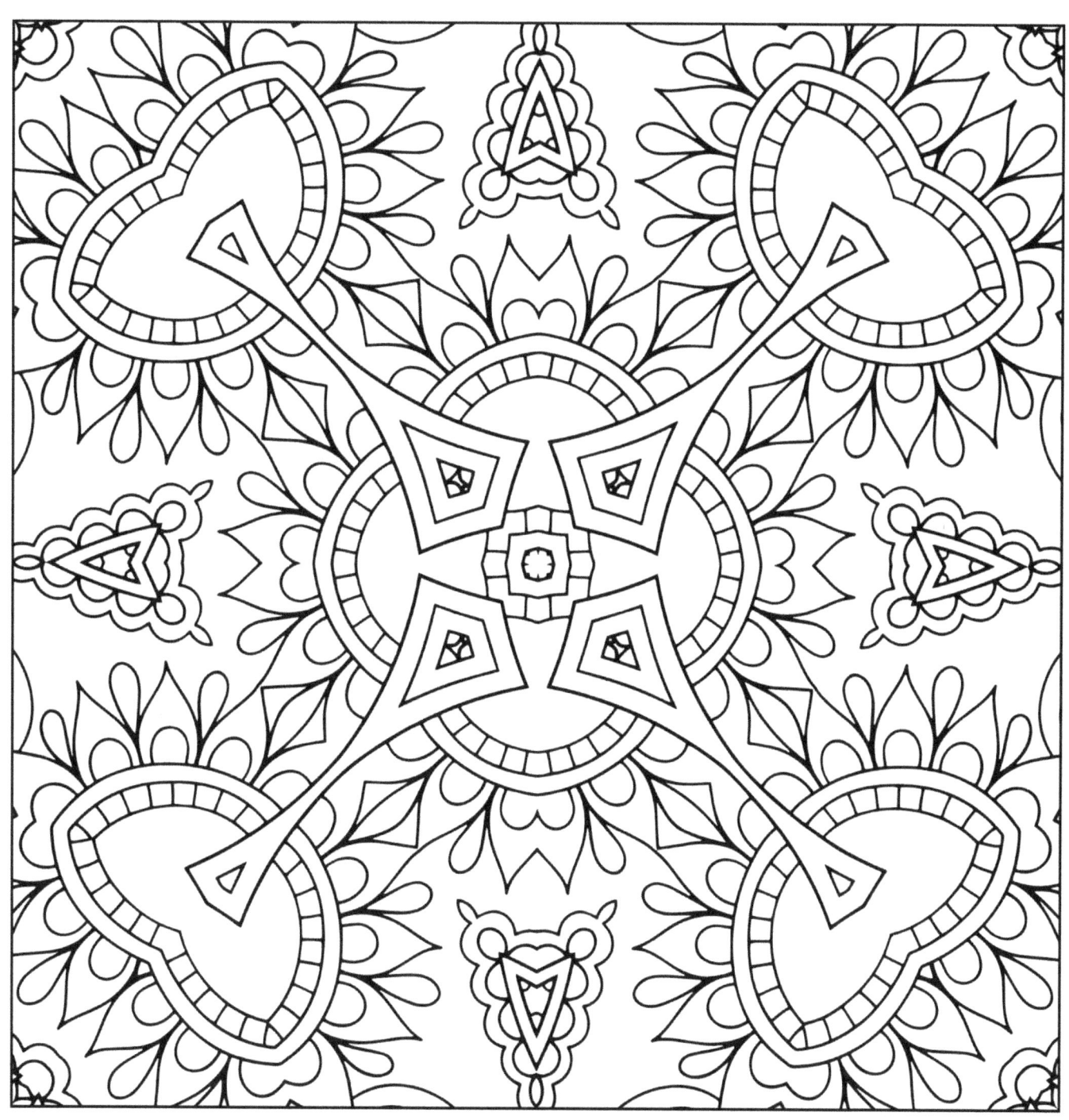

The problem is not the problem. The problem is your attitude about the problem. ~ Johnny Depp

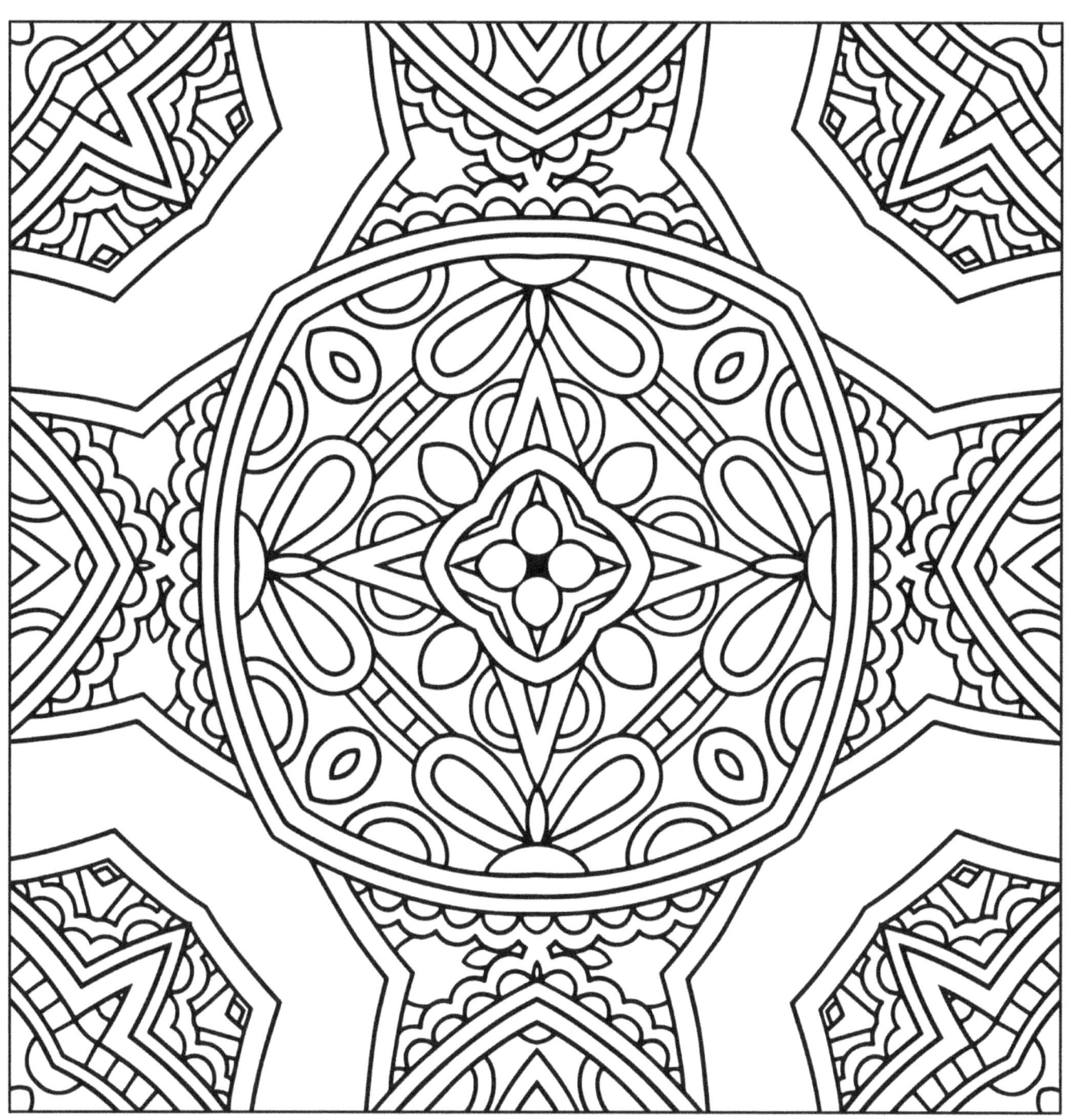

If there ever comes a day when we can't be together, keep me in your heart, I'll stay there forever.
~ Winnie the Pooh

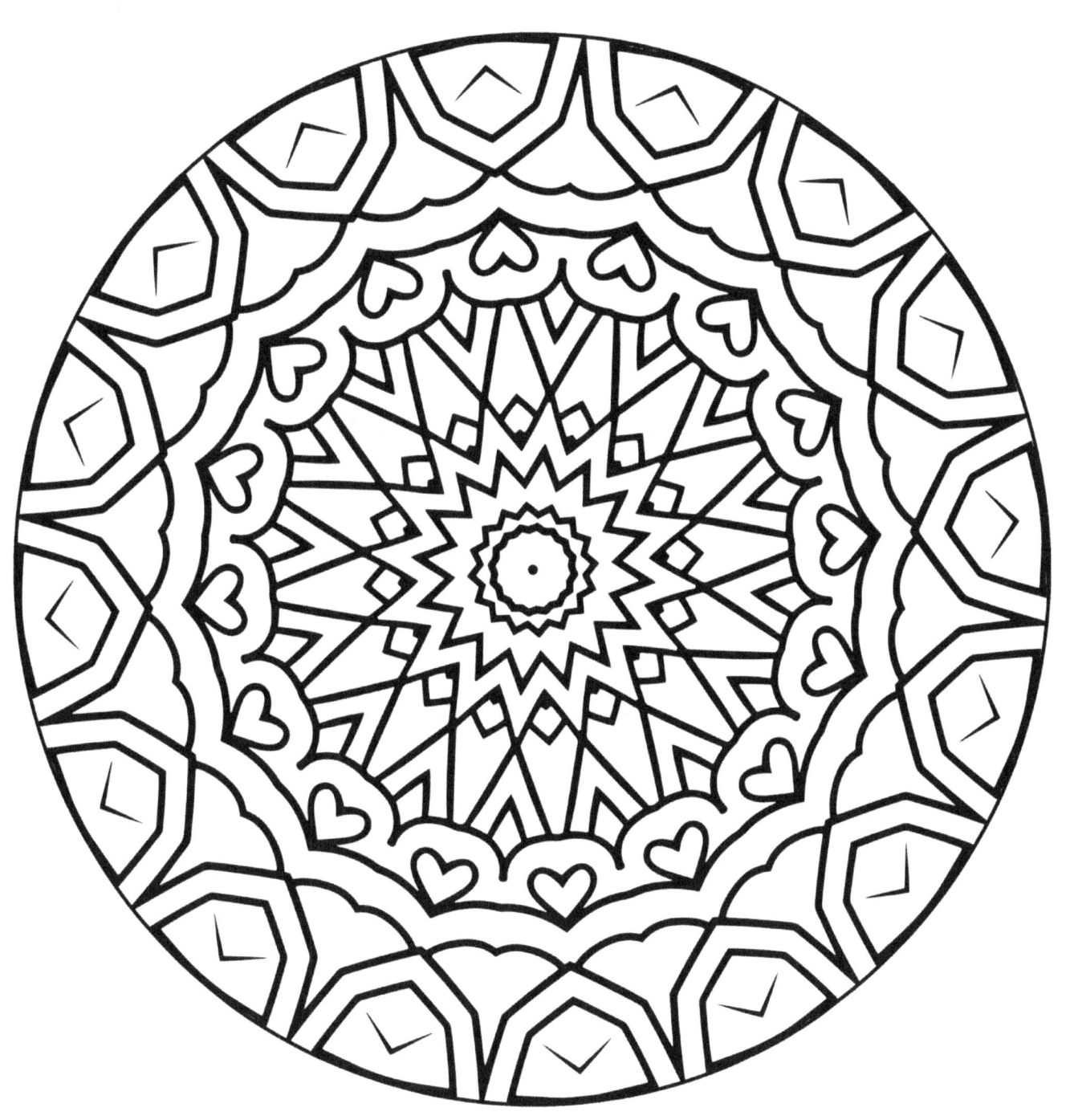

Live as if you were to die tomorrow.
Learn as if you were to live forever.
~ Mahatma Gandhi

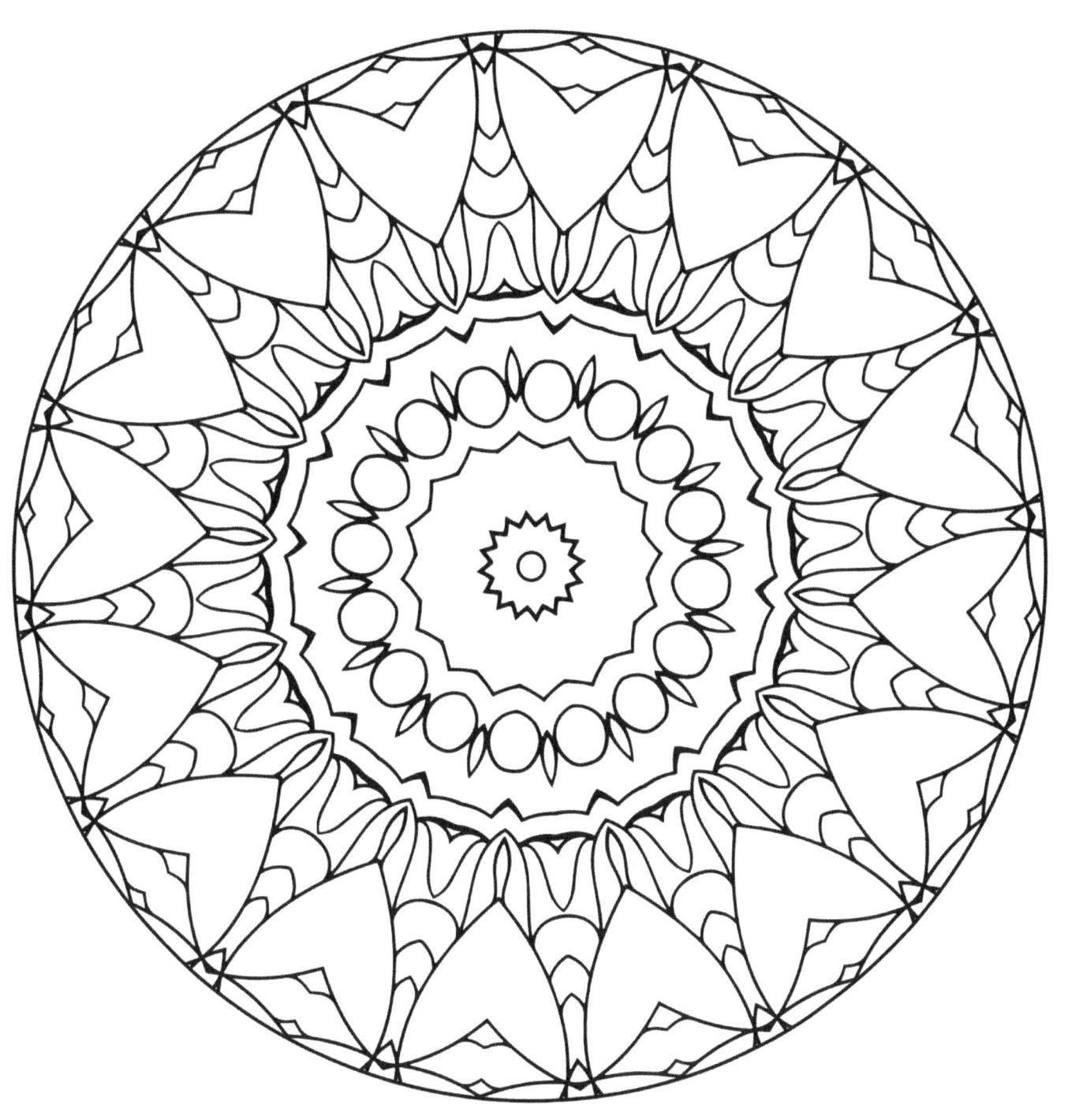

You can't stay in your corner of the forest waiting for others to come to you. You have to go to them sometimes. ~ Winnie the Pooh

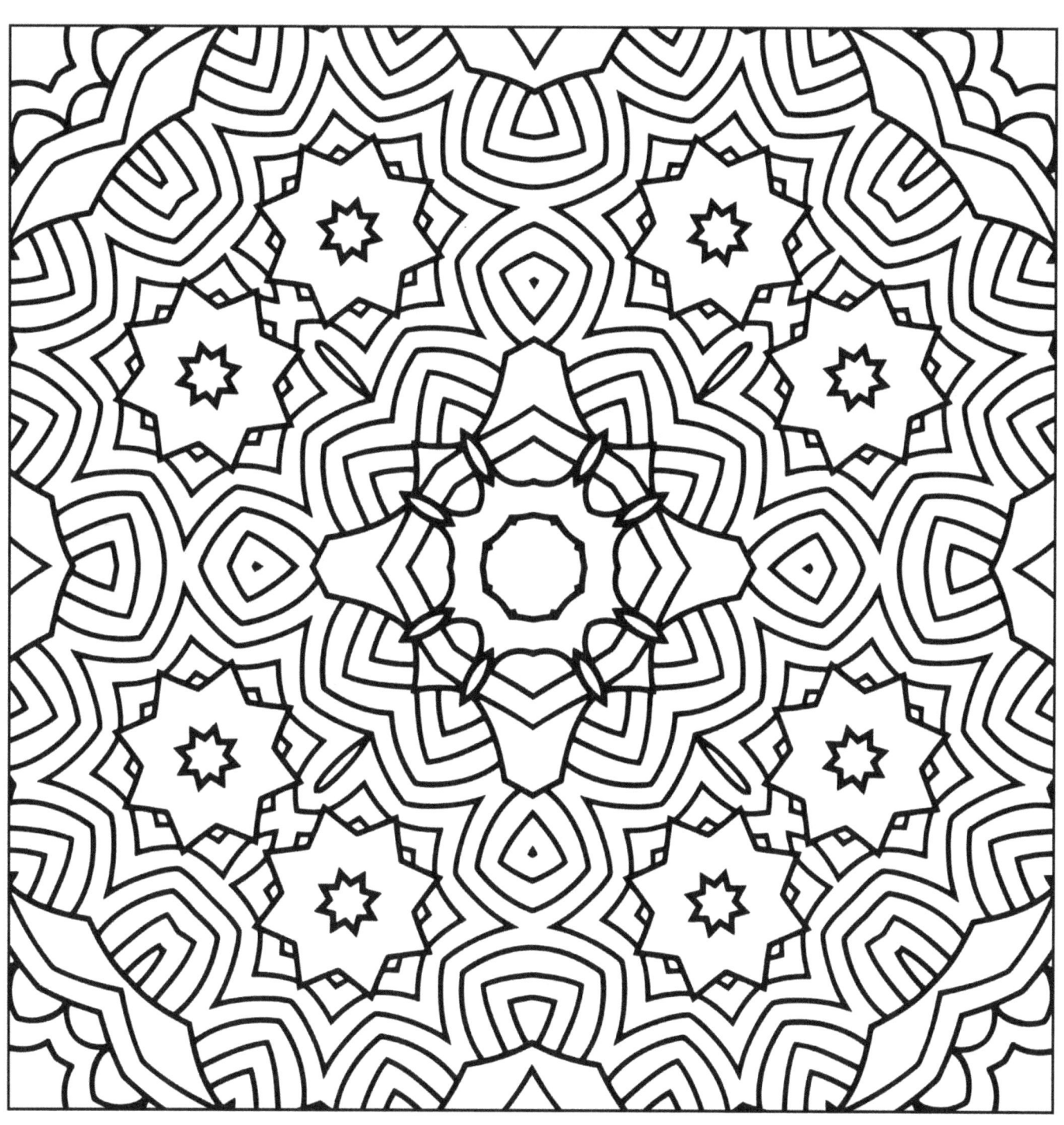

If you want to live a happy life tie it
to a goal. Not to people or things.
~ Albert Einstein

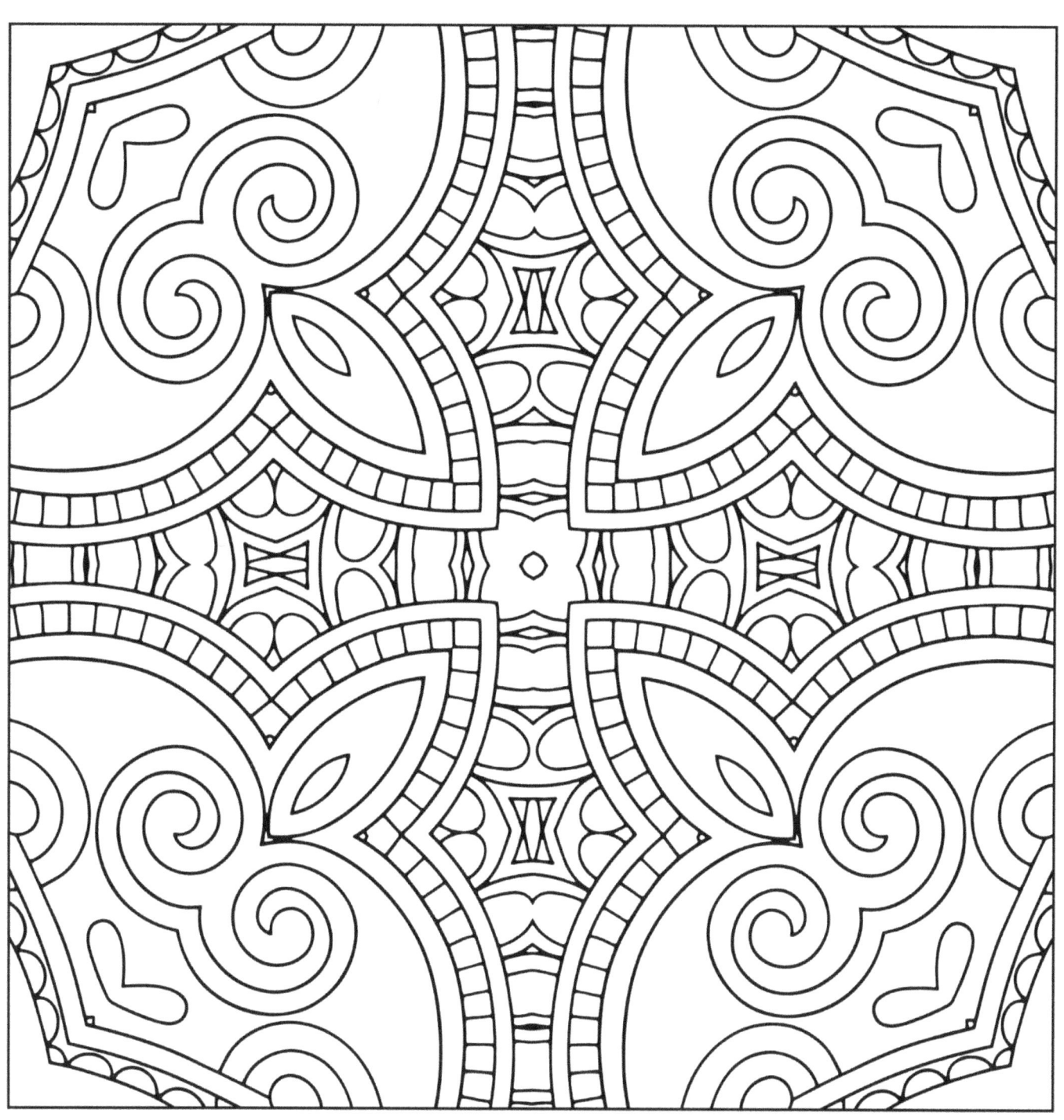

Once in awhile someone amazing comes along, and here I am. ~Tigger

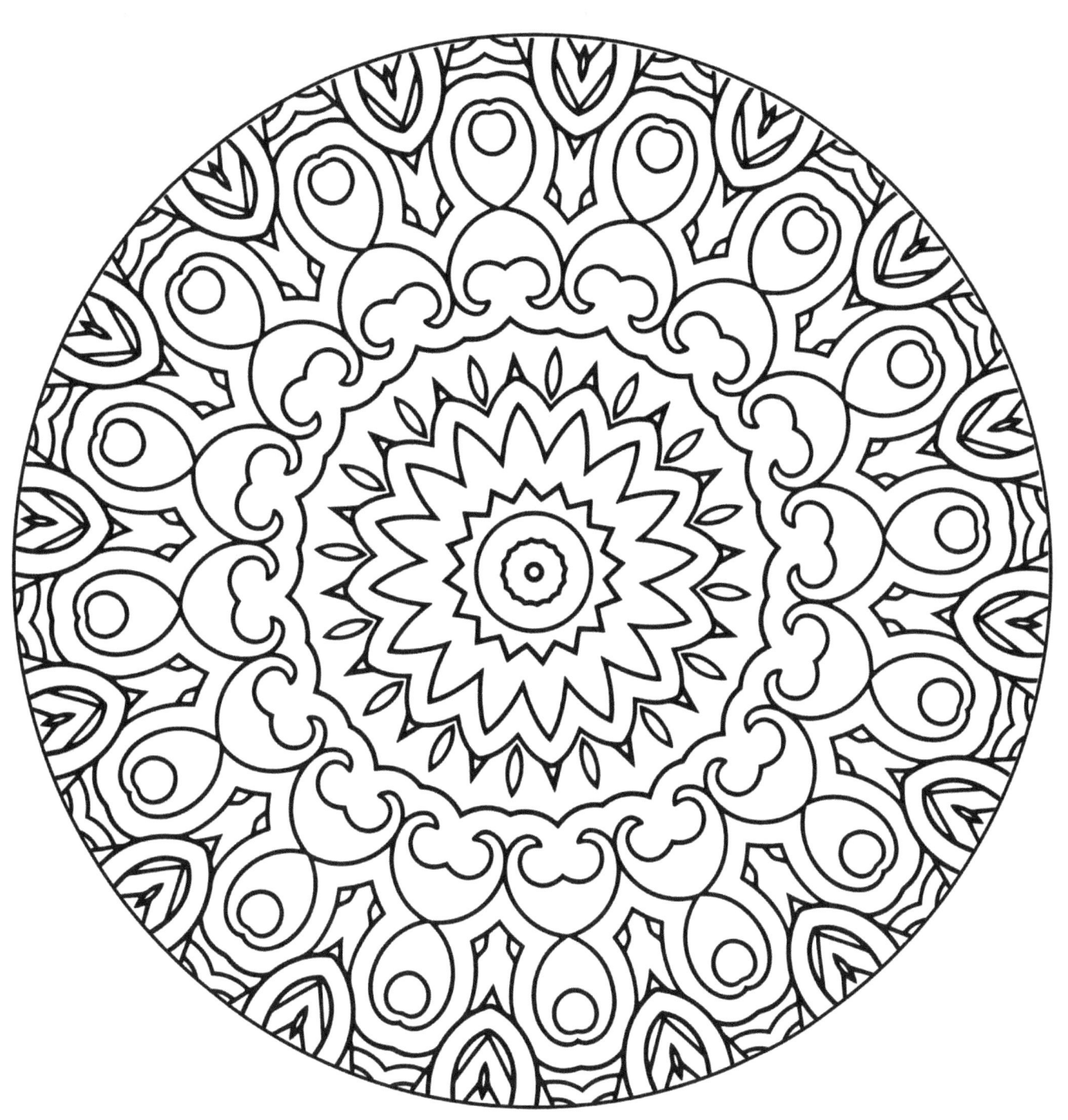

Honesty is a very expensive gift. Do not expect it from cheap people.
~ Warren Buffet

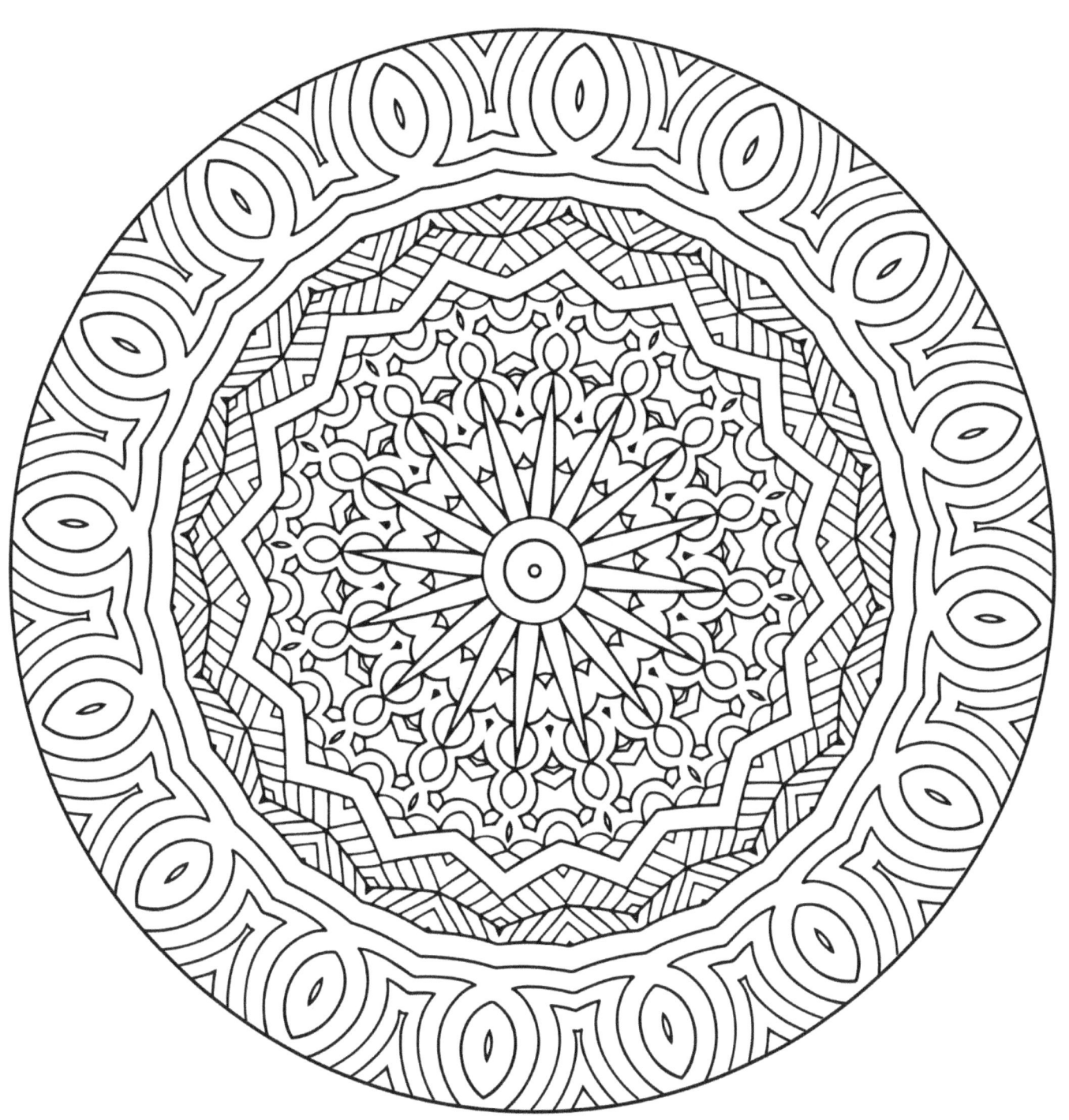

Me, I'm dishonest, and you can always trust a dishonest person to be dishonest. Honestly it's the honest ones you have to watch out for.

~ Johnny Depp

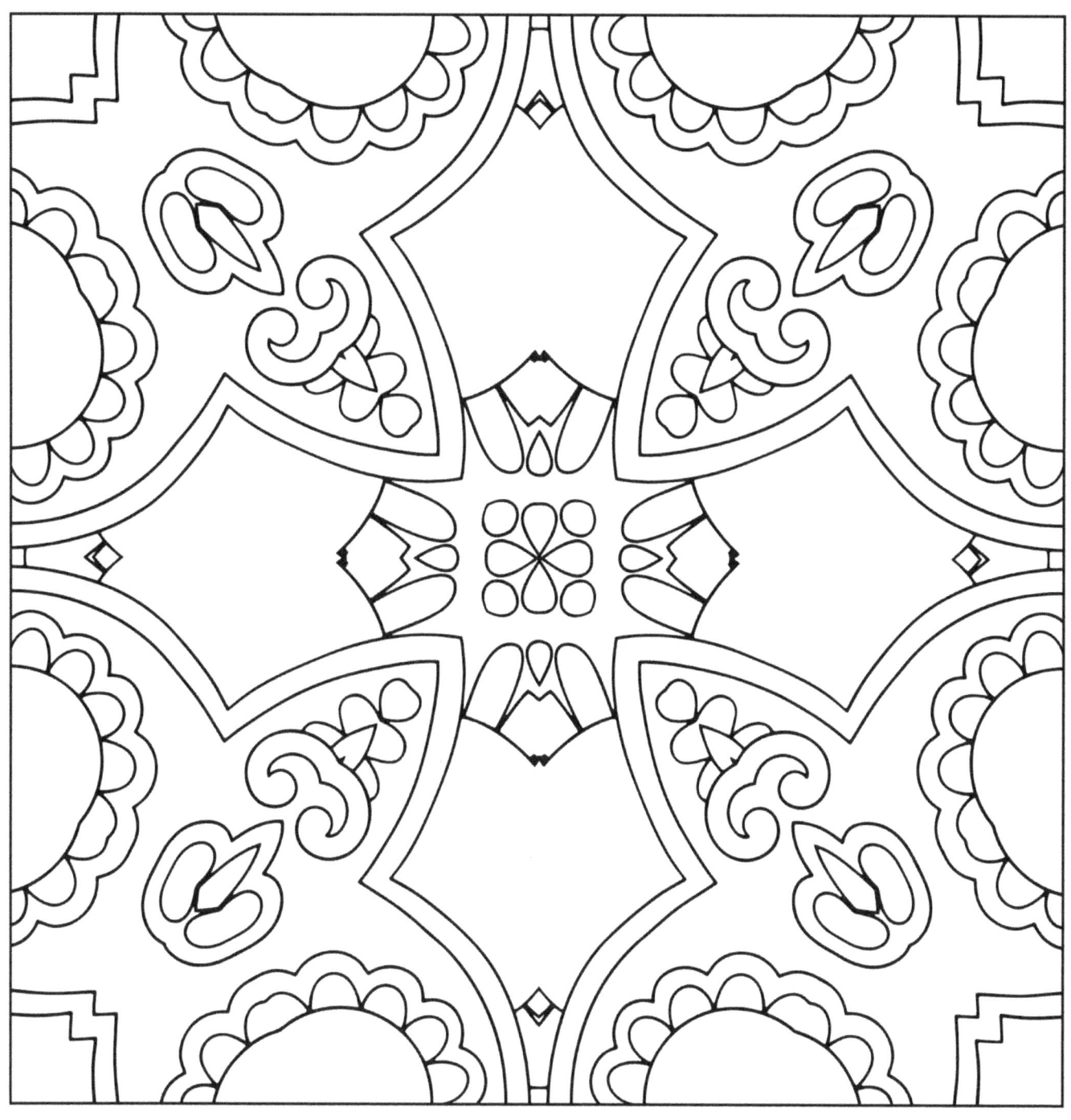

If you live to be 100, I want to live to be 100 minus a day so I never have to live without you.

~ Winnie the Pooh

Kind words are short and easy to speak, but their echoes are truly endless. ~ Mother Teresa

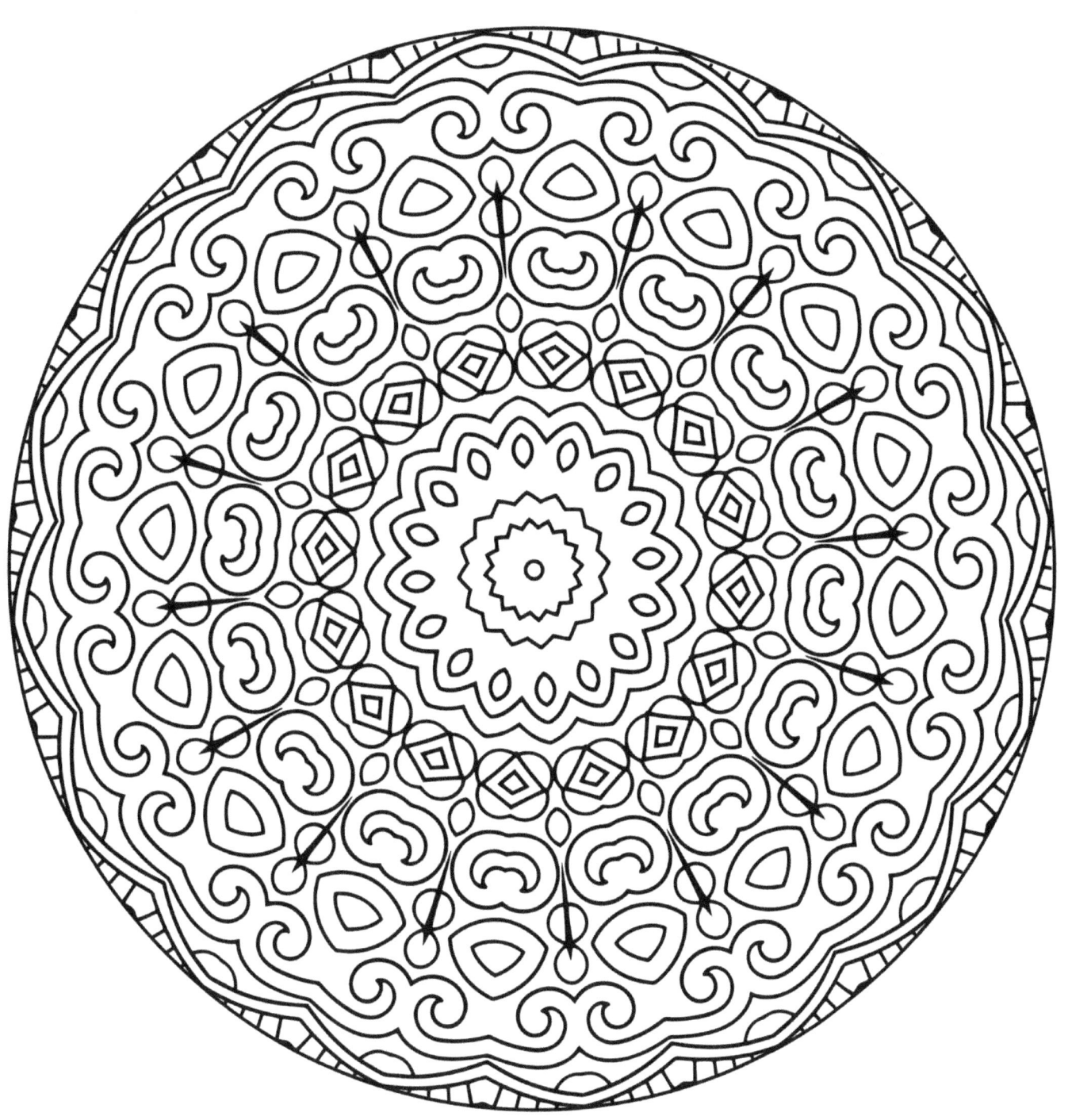

The only way to do great work is to love what you do. ~Steve Jobs

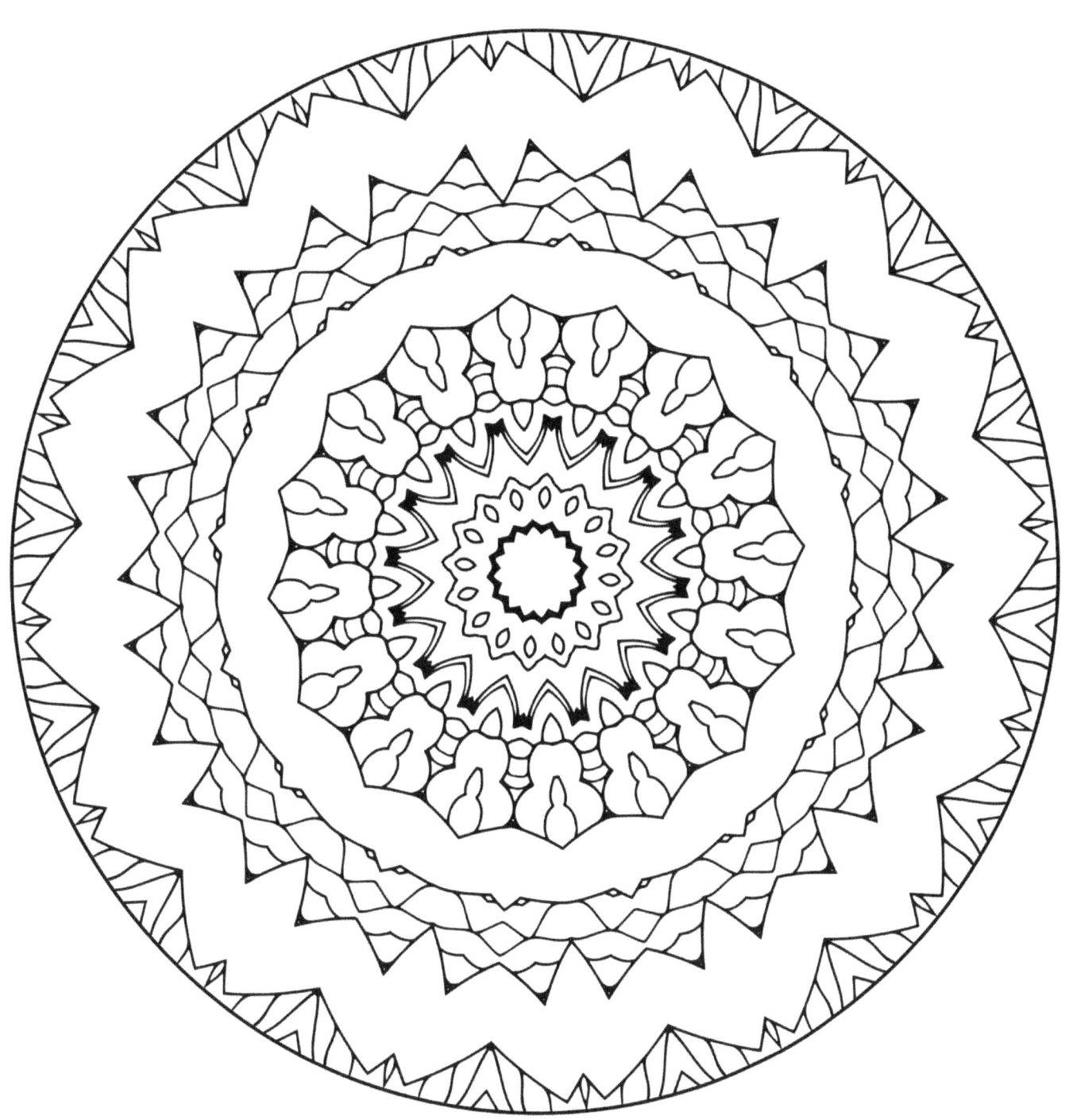

Dream as if you'll live forever, live
as if you will die today.
~ James Dean

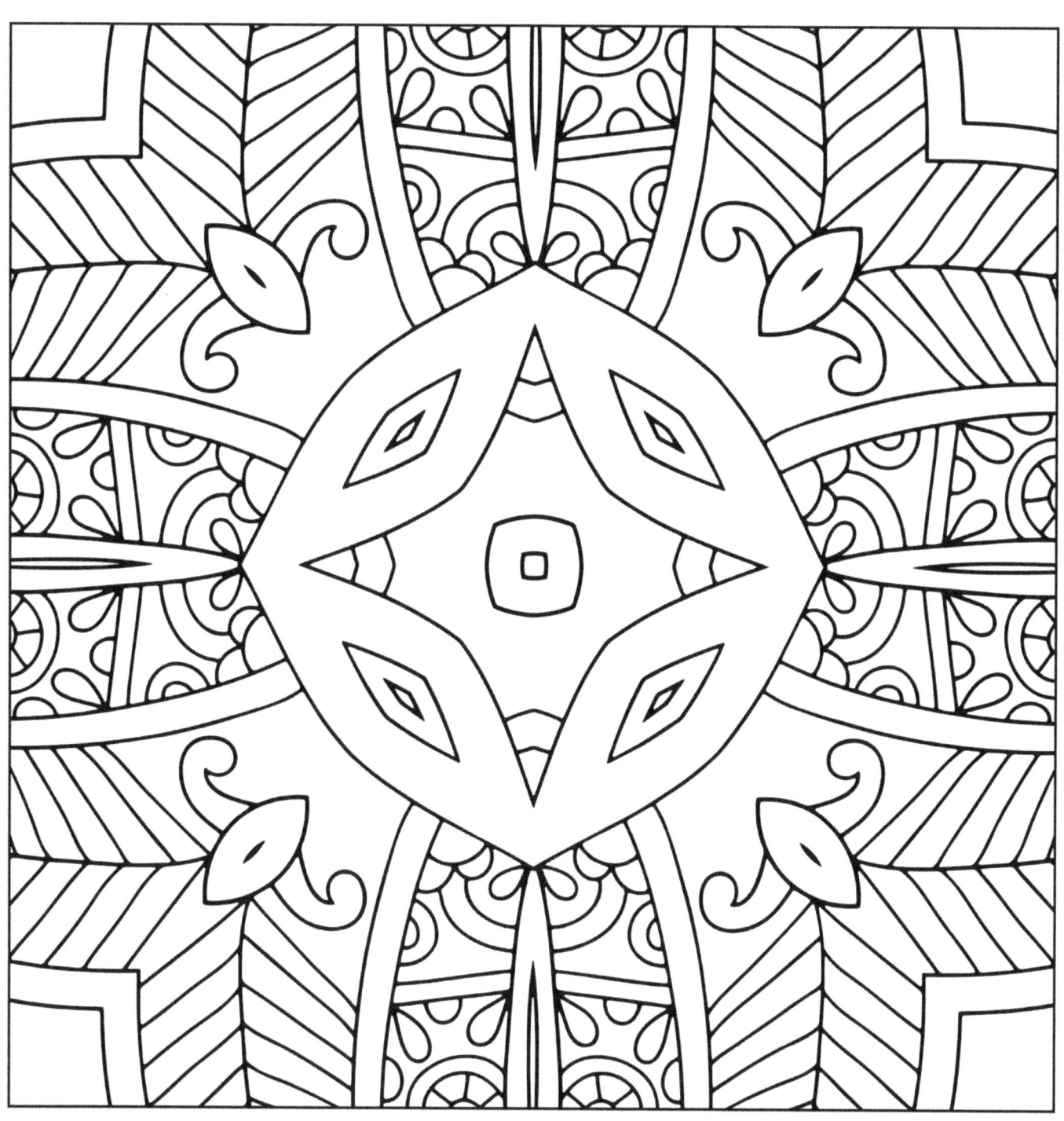

I'm the one that's got to die when it's time for me to die, so let me live my life the way I want to.

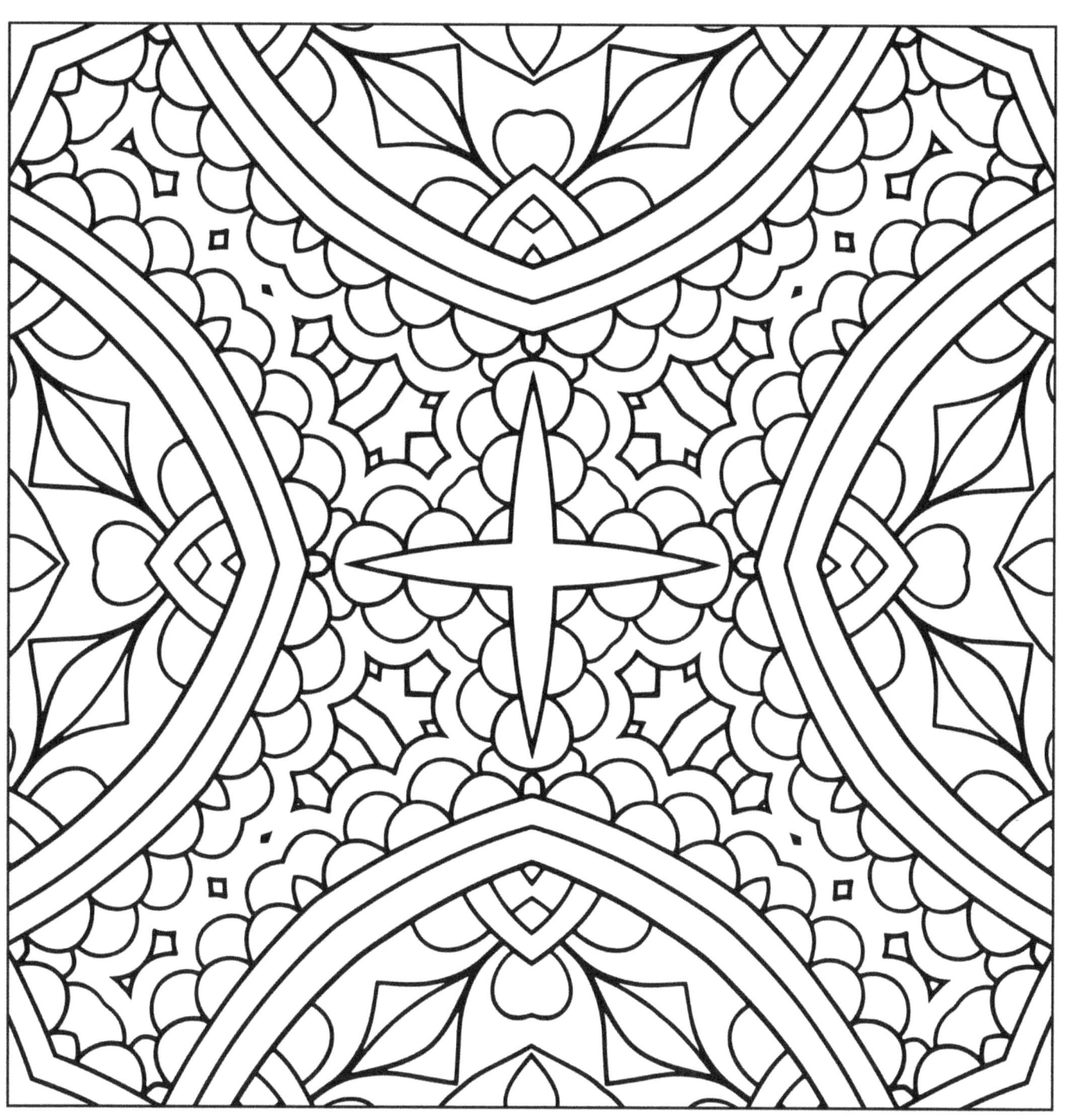

You're only given a little spark of madness. You mustn't lose it.

~ Robin Williams

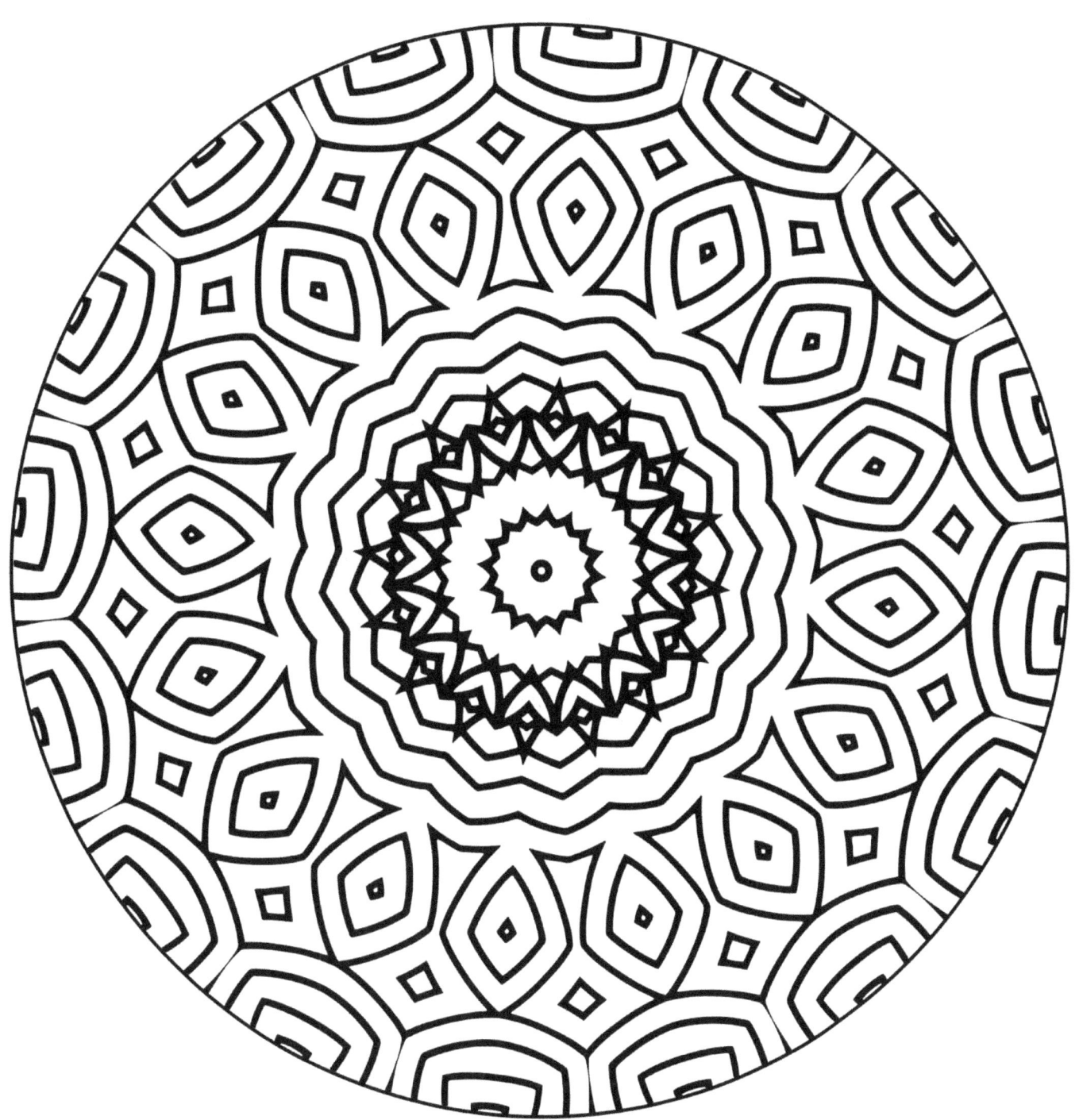

The best way to cheer yourself up

is to cheer someone else up.

~ Mark Twain

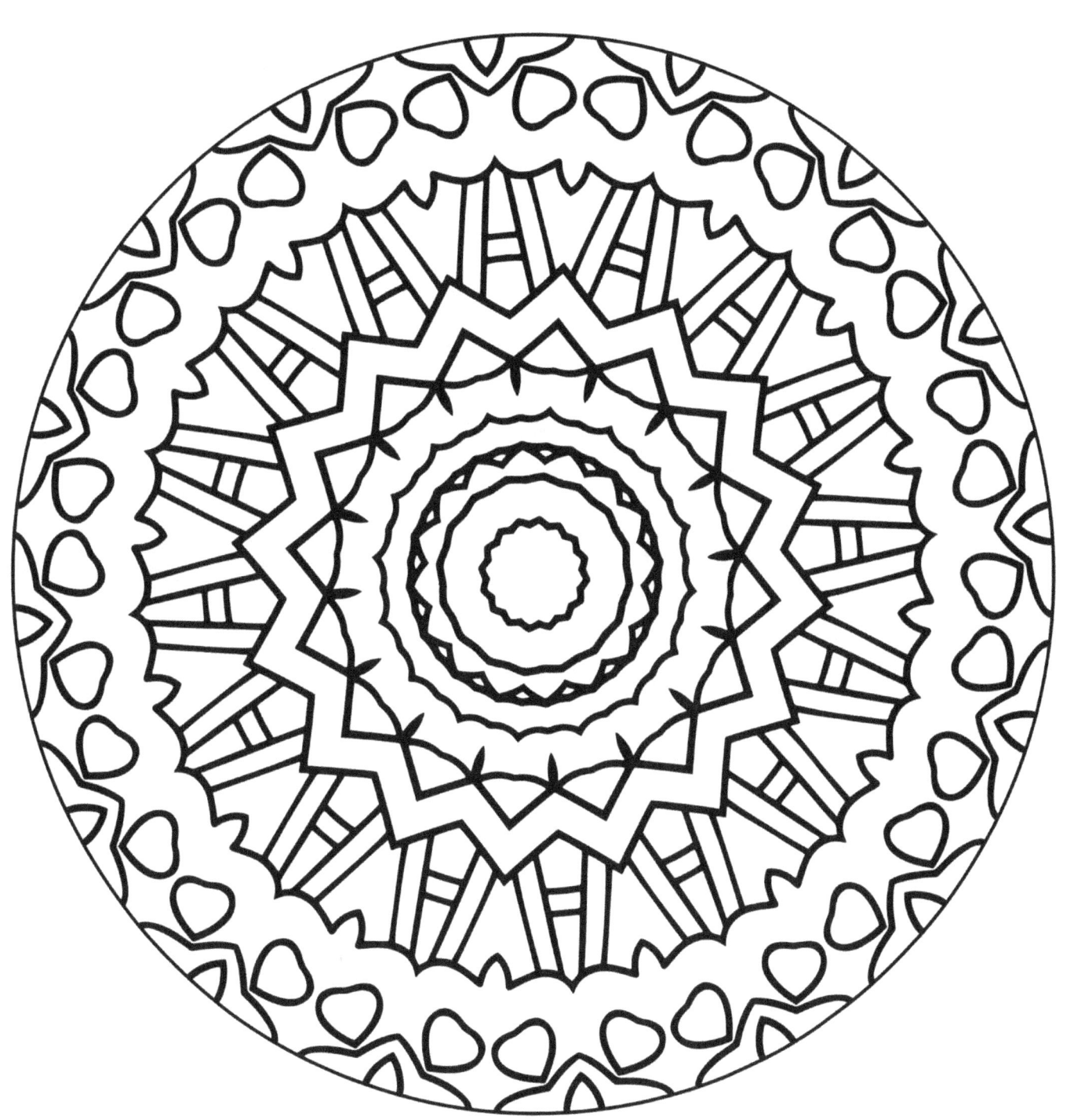

I've just got to maintain my passion for what I do. ~Leonardo DiCaprio

Two things are infinite; the universe and stupidity. ...And I'm not sure about the universe.

~Albert Einstein

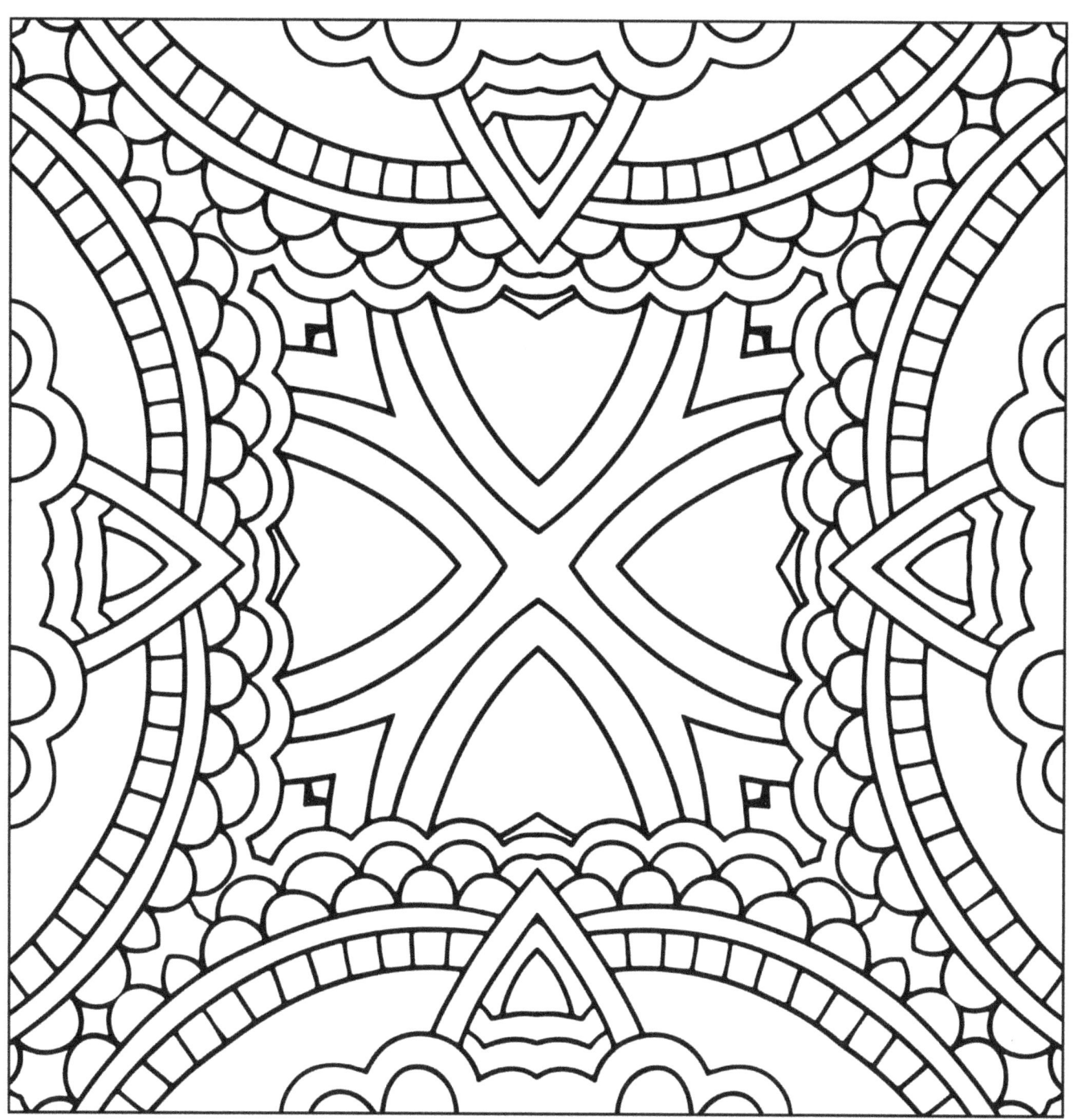

Do not judge me by my successes, judge me by how many times I fell down and got back up again.

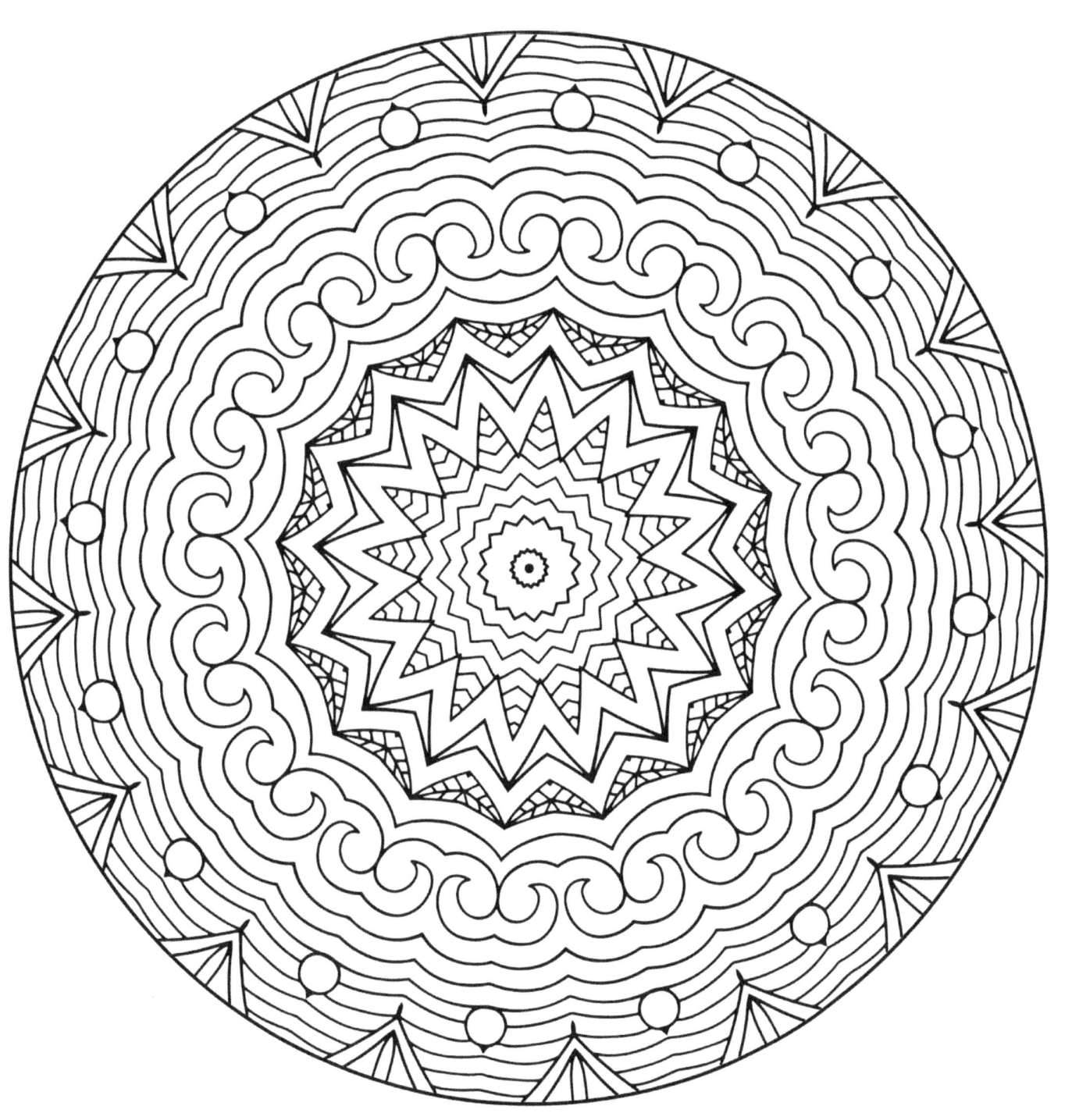

If you can dream it you can do it.
~ Walt Disney

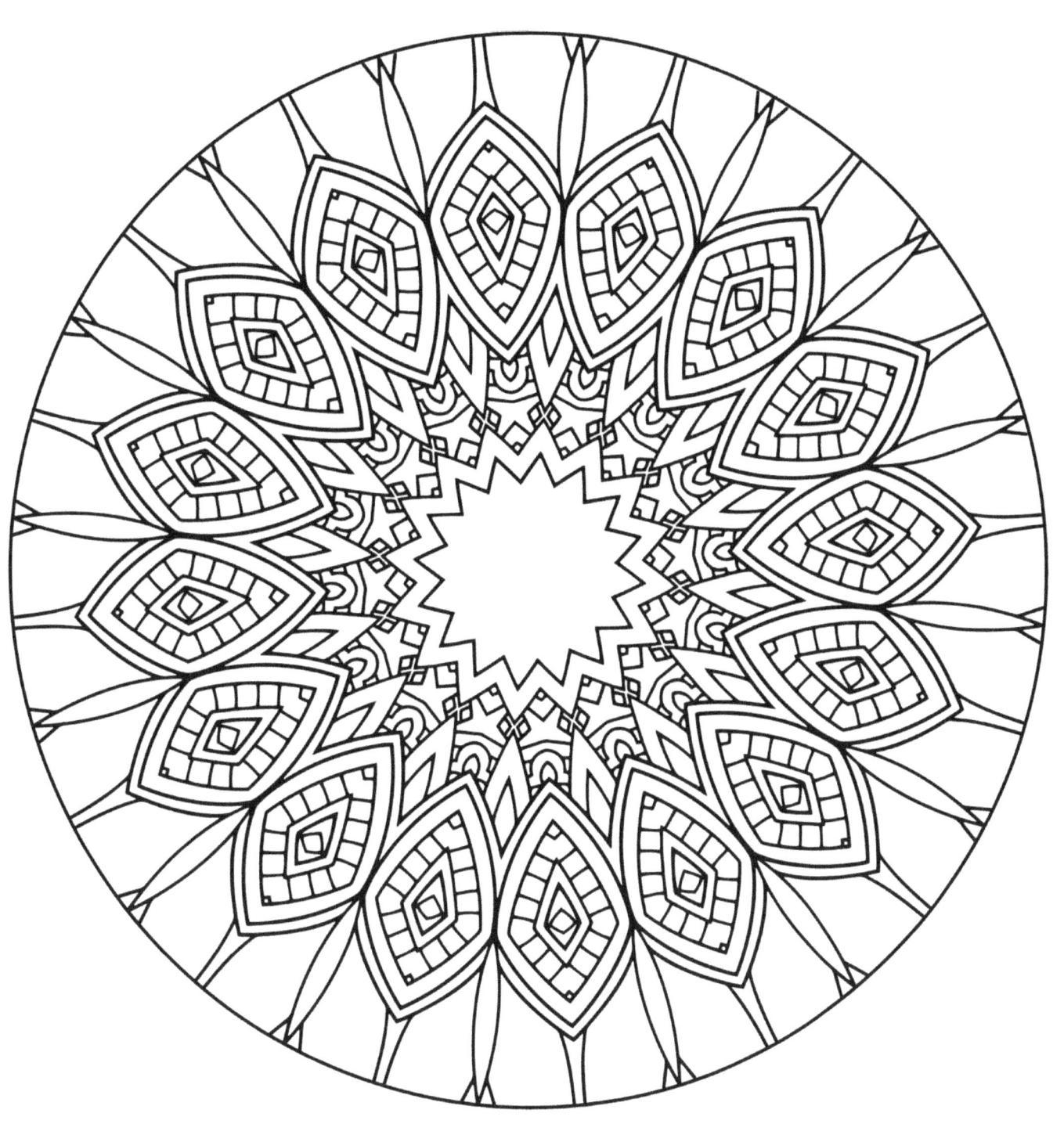

No matter how hard the past, you can always begin again. ~Buddha

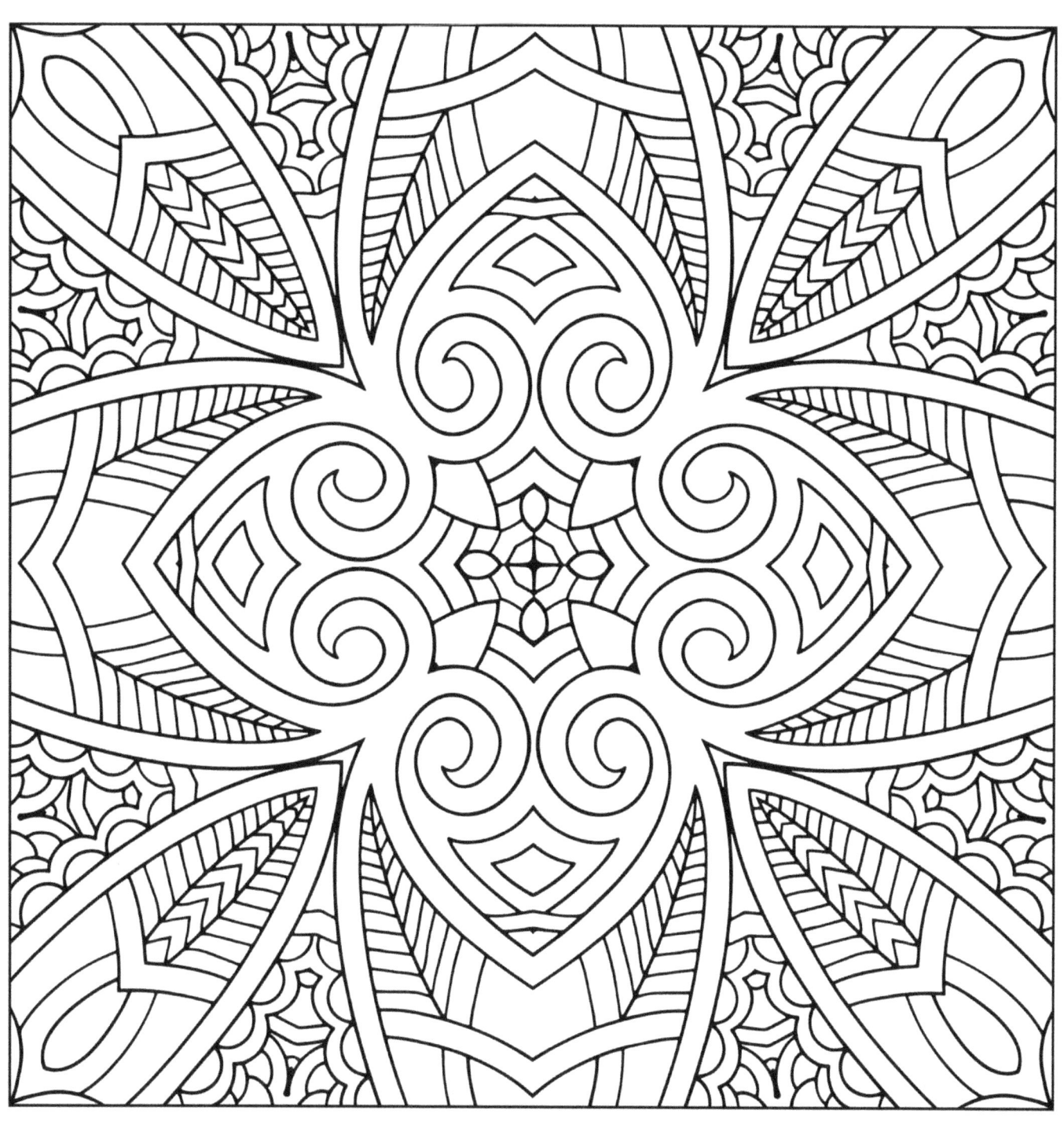

The future depends on what we do in the present. ~ Mahatma Gandhi

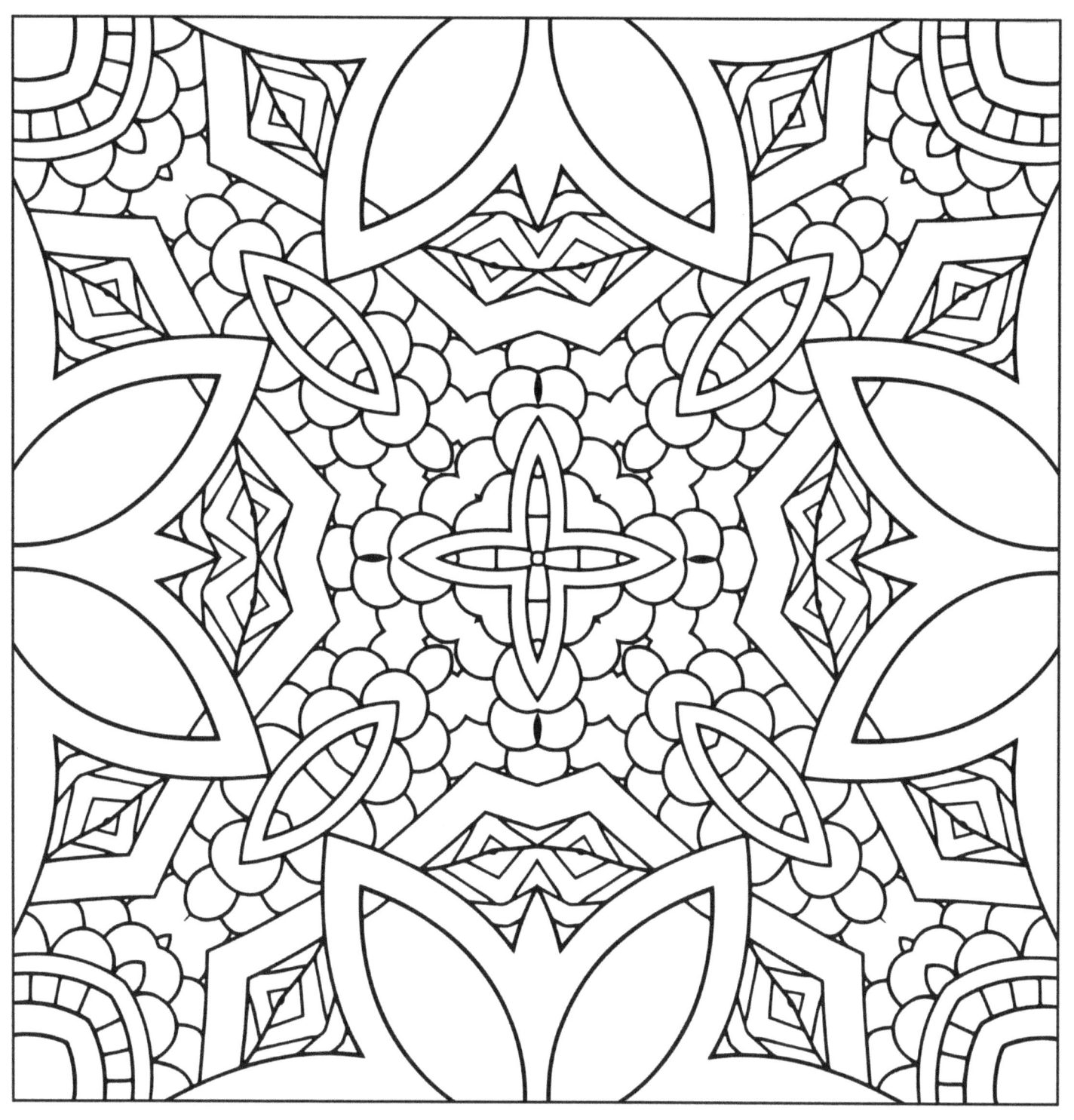

We all want to be famous people, and the moment we want to be something is the moment we are no longer free.
~ Jiddu Krishnamurti

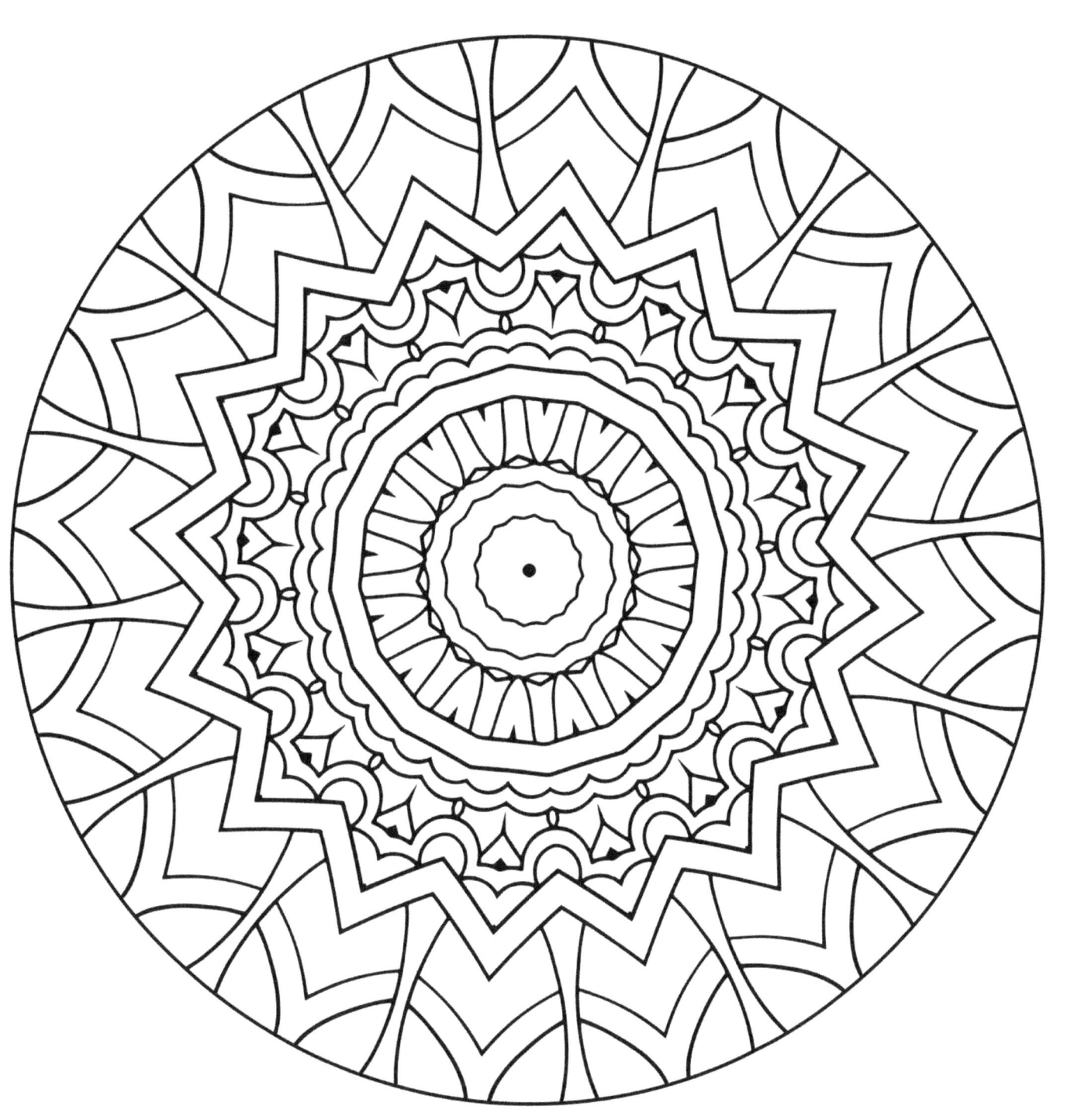

Imagination is everything. It is the preview of life's coming attractions.
~Albert Einstein

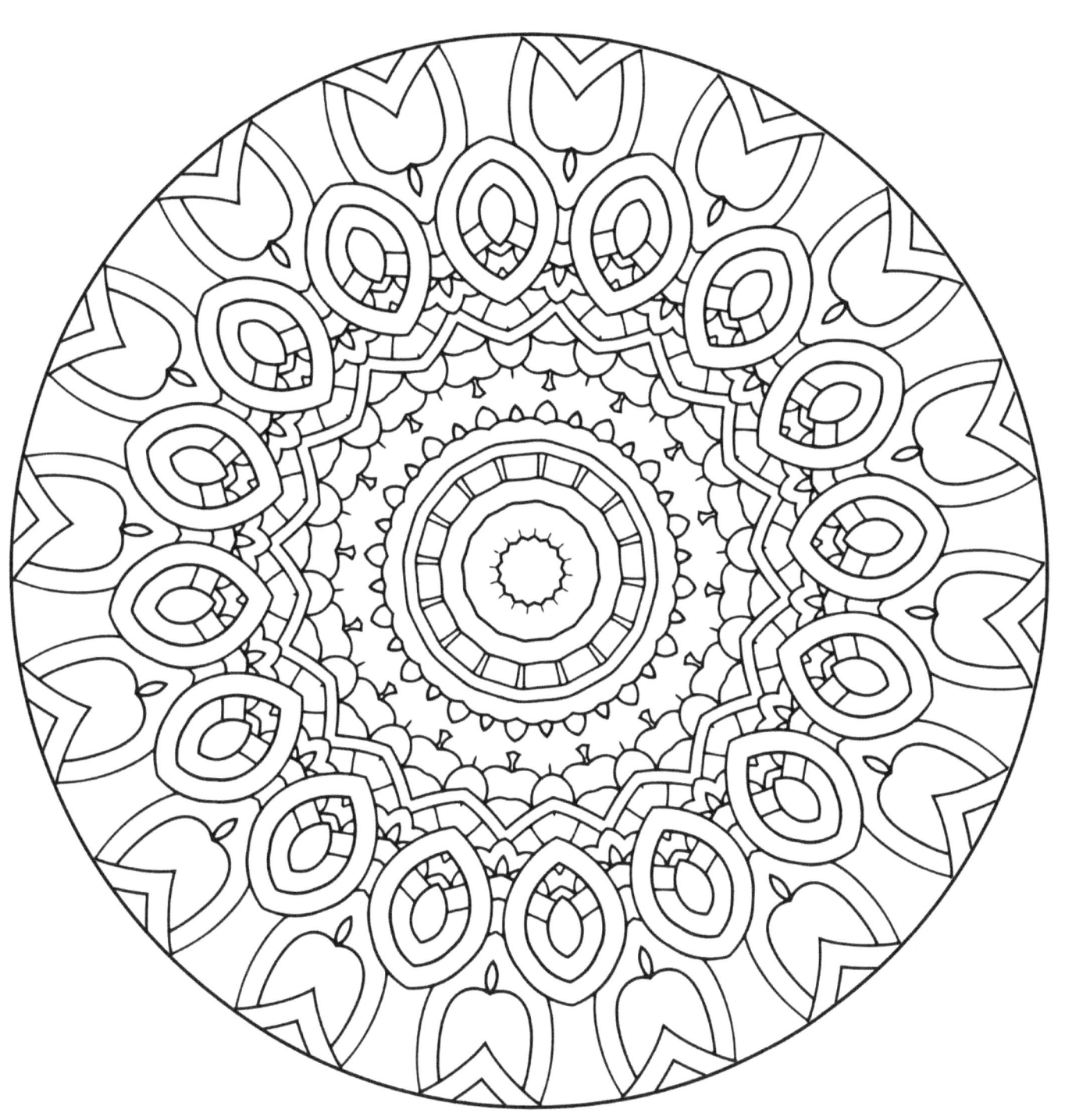

It isn't the mountains ahead to climb that wear you down. It's the pebble in your shoe. ~ Muhammad Ali

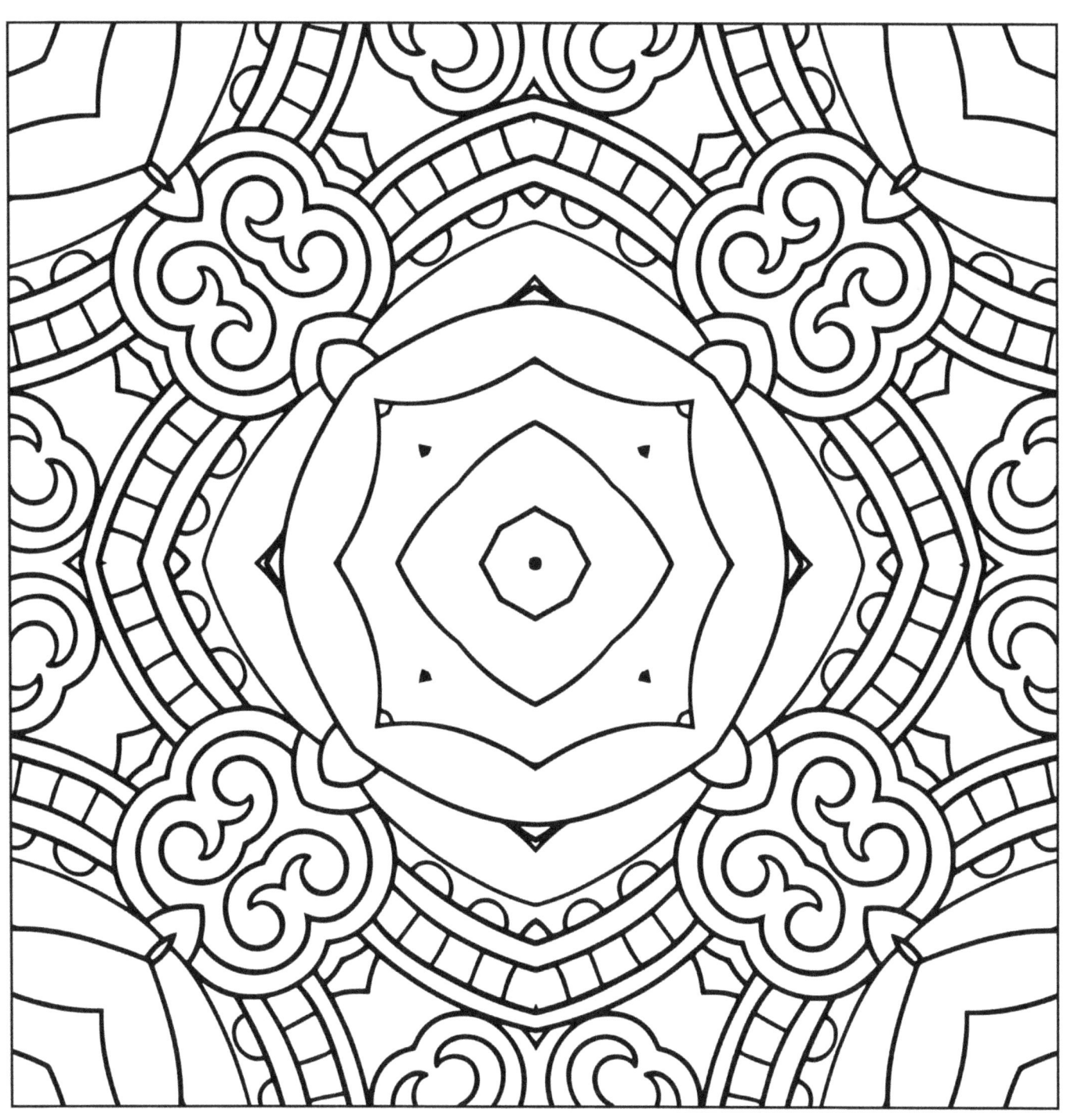

If you realize that all things change, there is nothing you will try to hold onto. If you are not afraid of dying, there is nothing you cannot achieve.
~Lao Tzu

A fool thinks himself to be wise, but a wise man knows himself to be a fool. ~ William Shakespear

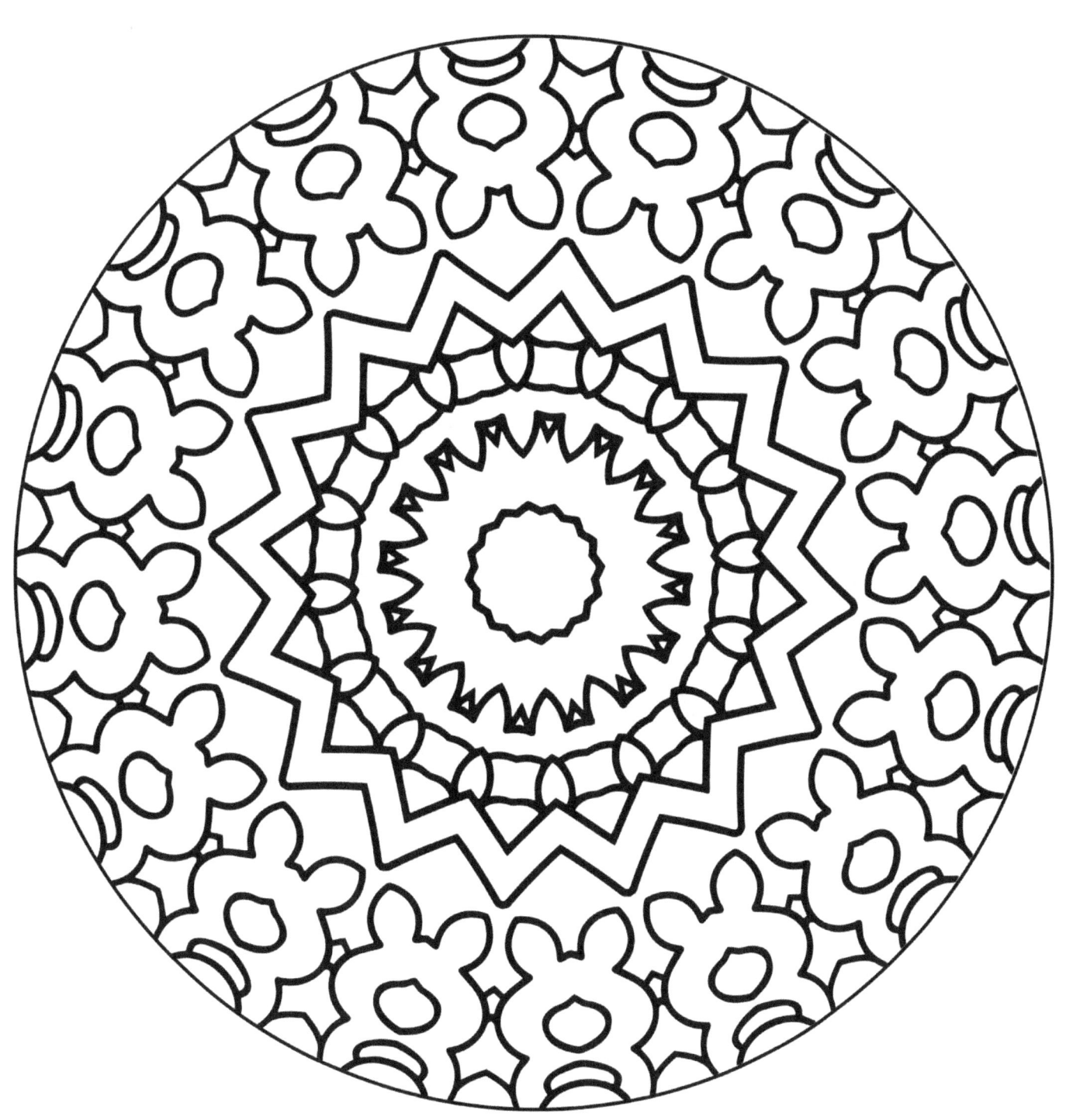

The ones who are crazy enough to think that they can change the world, are the ones who do.

~ Steve Jobs

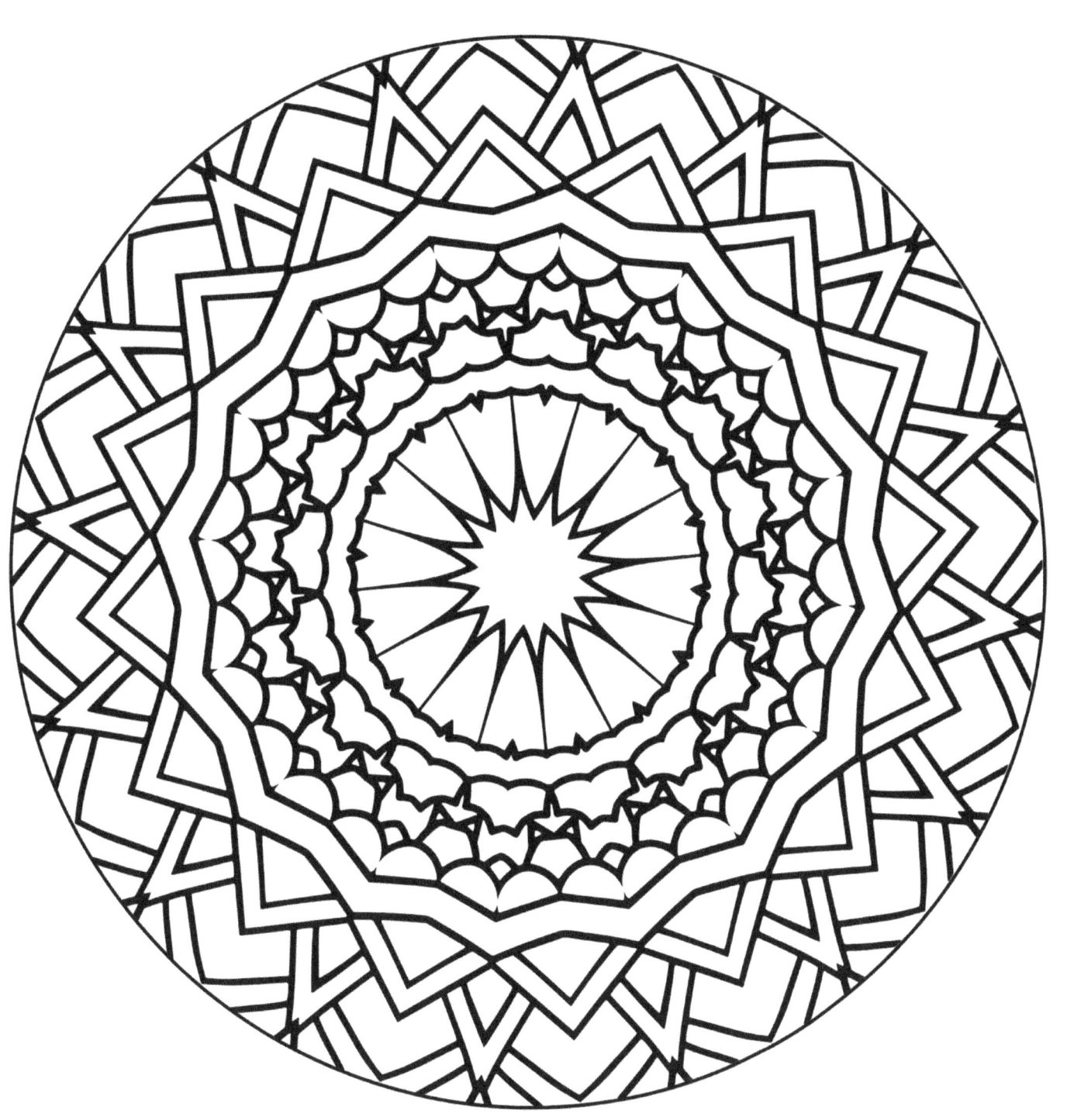

Happiness does not depend on what you have or who you are. It solely relies on what you think. ~Buddha

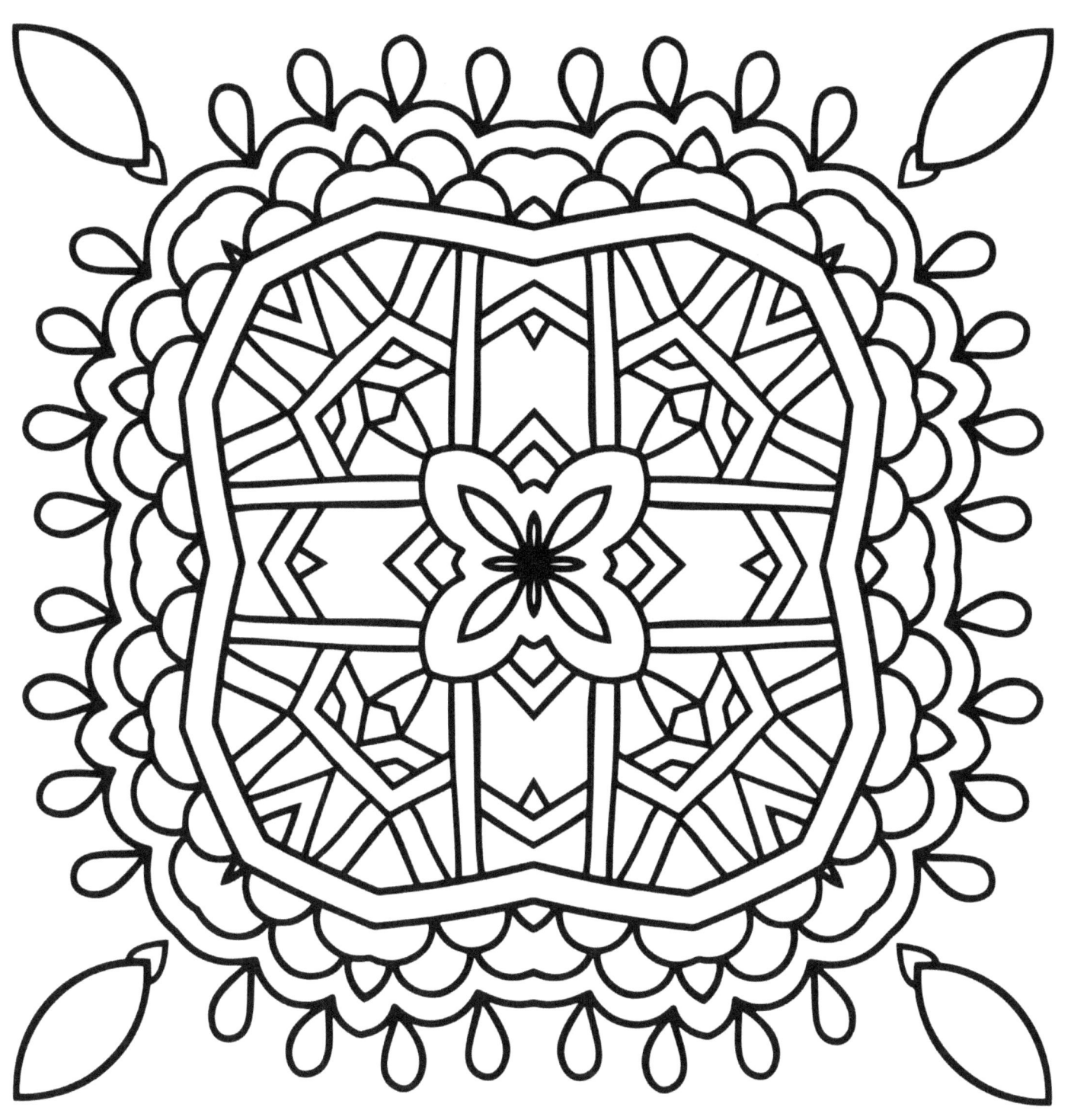

If I had asked people what they wanted they would have said faster horses. ~Henry Ford

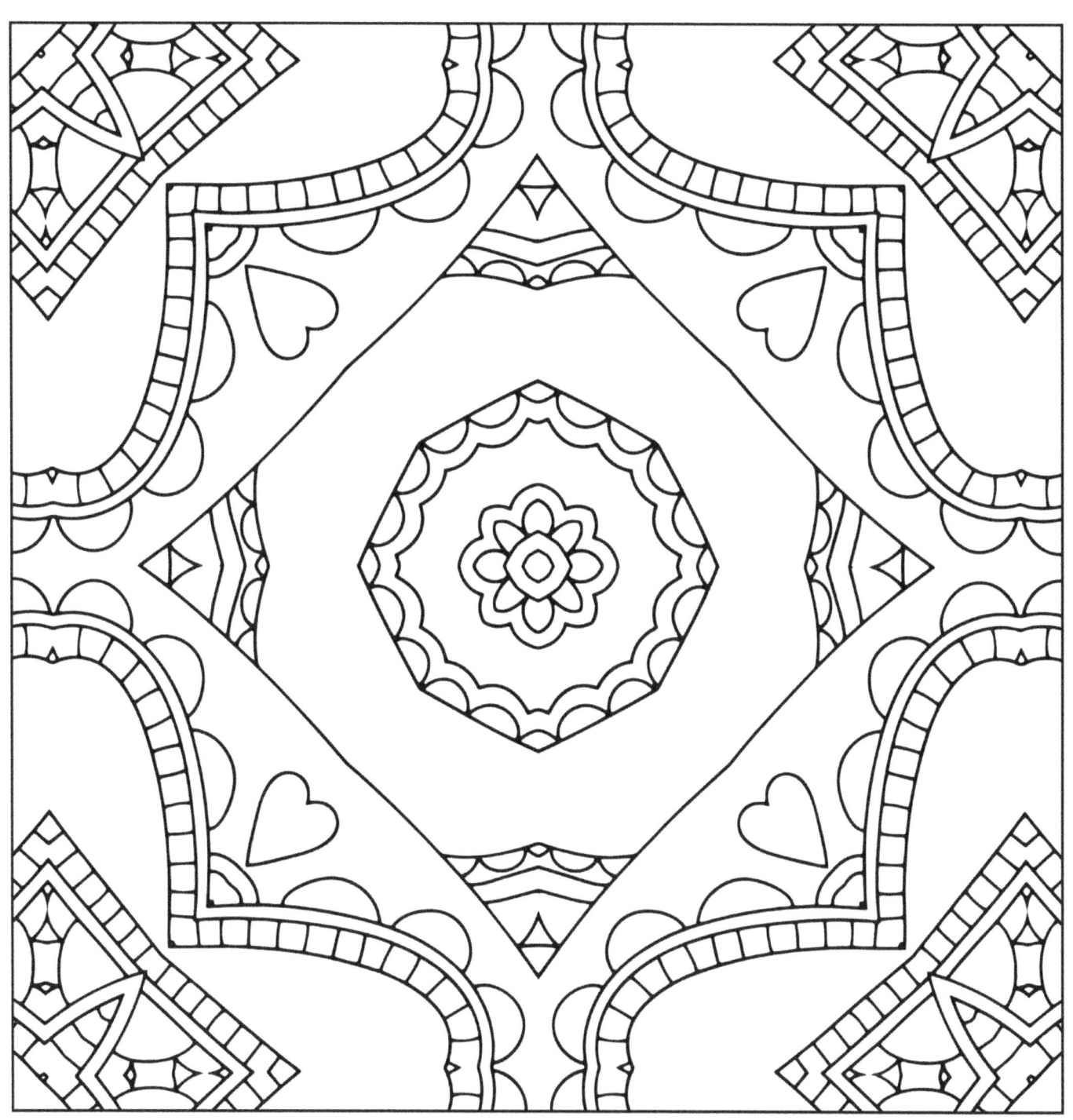

Every child is an artist, the problem is staying an artist when you grow up. ~ Pablo Picasso

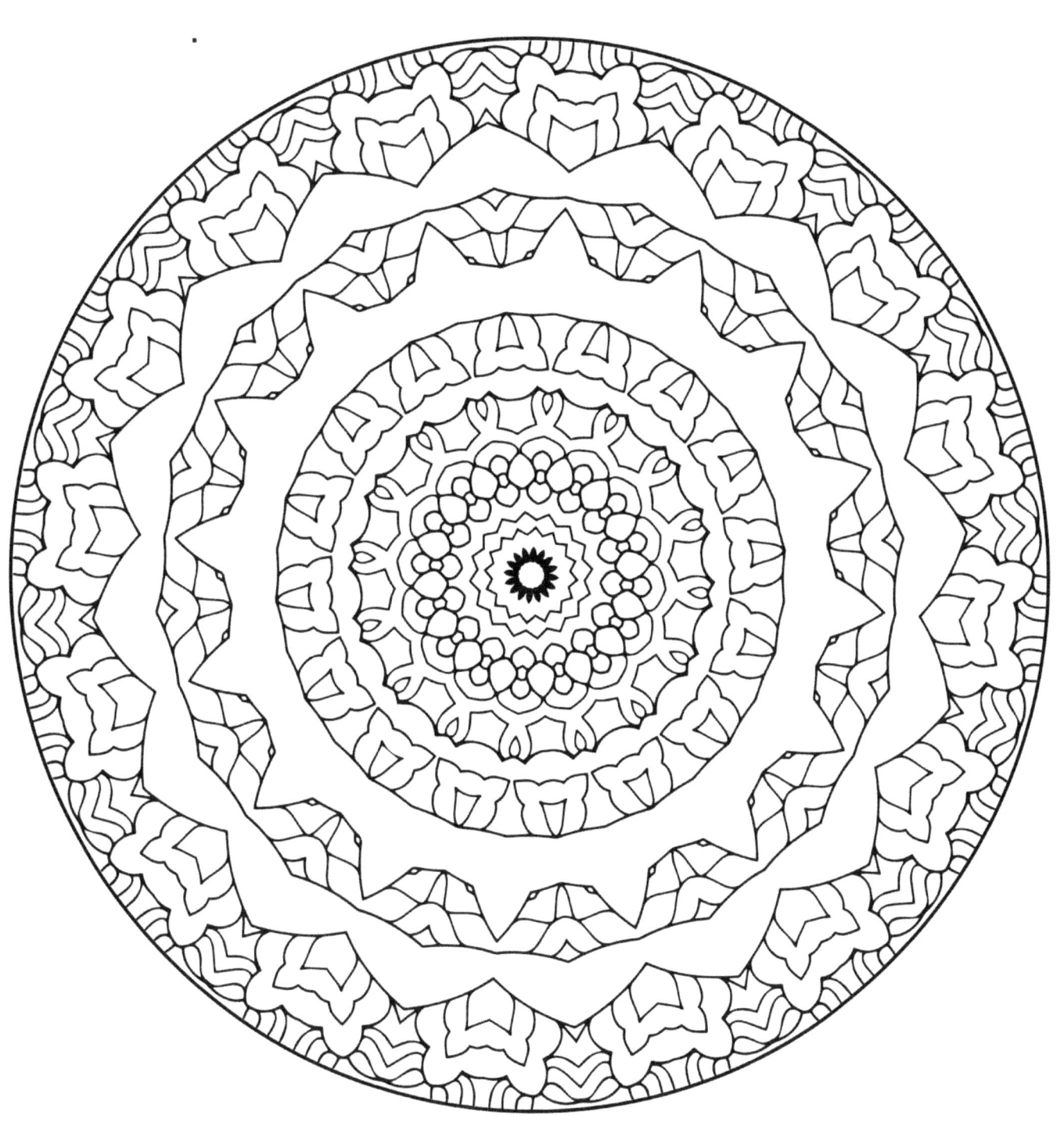

Time you enjoy wasting was not wasted.

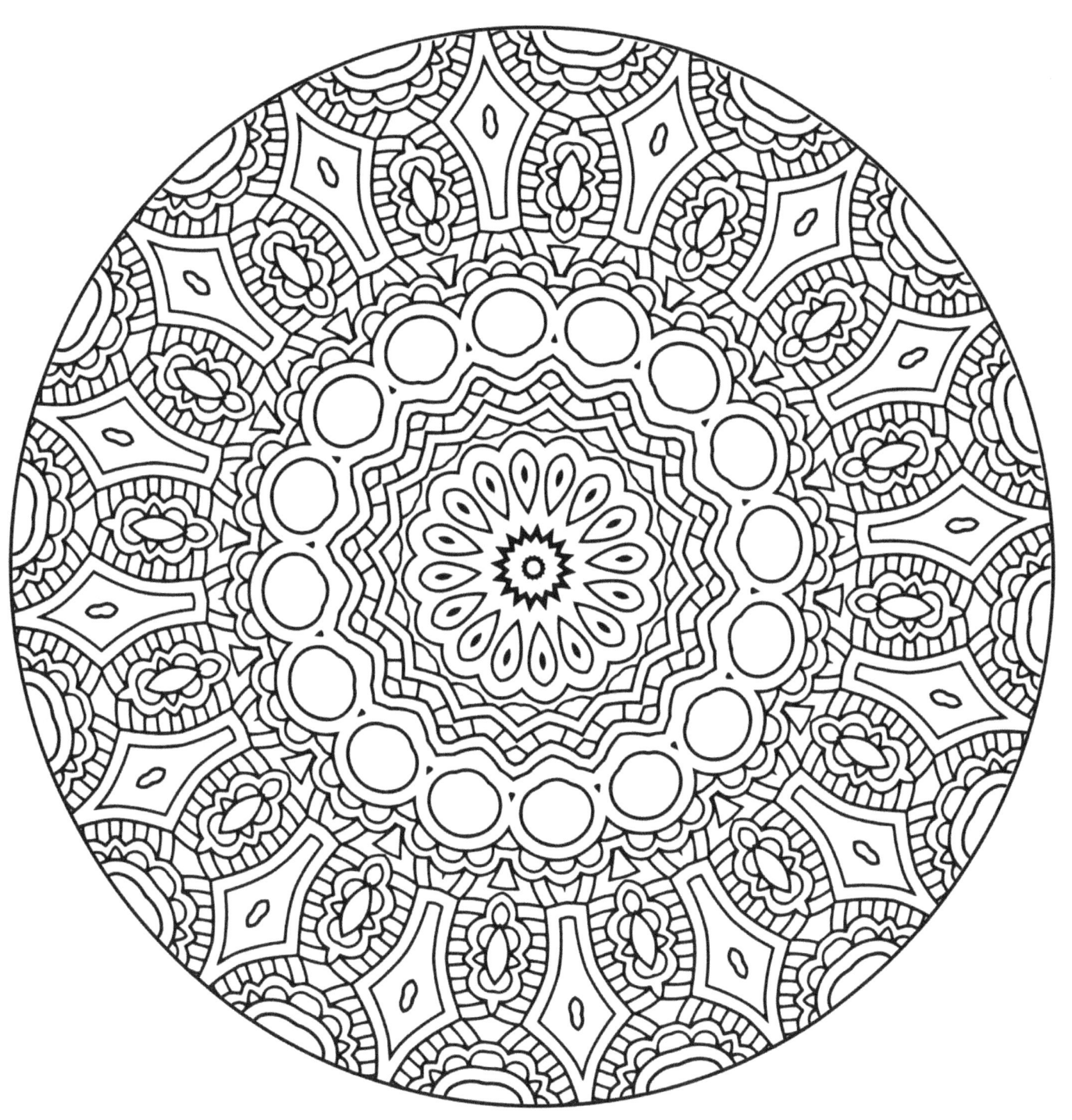

You can't beat the person who never gives up. ~Babe Ruth

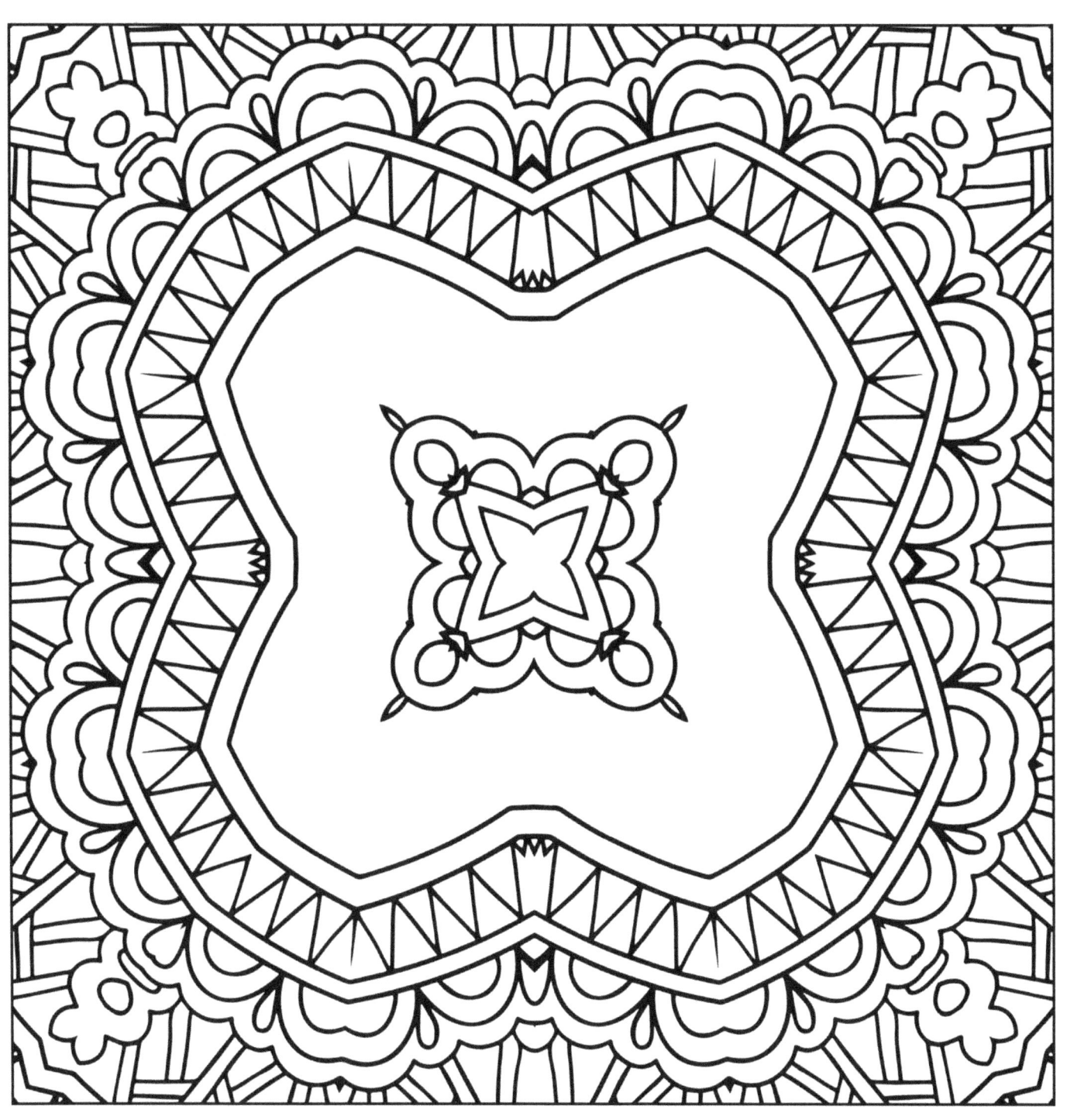

If you can't do great things then do small things in a great way.
~ Napoleon Hill

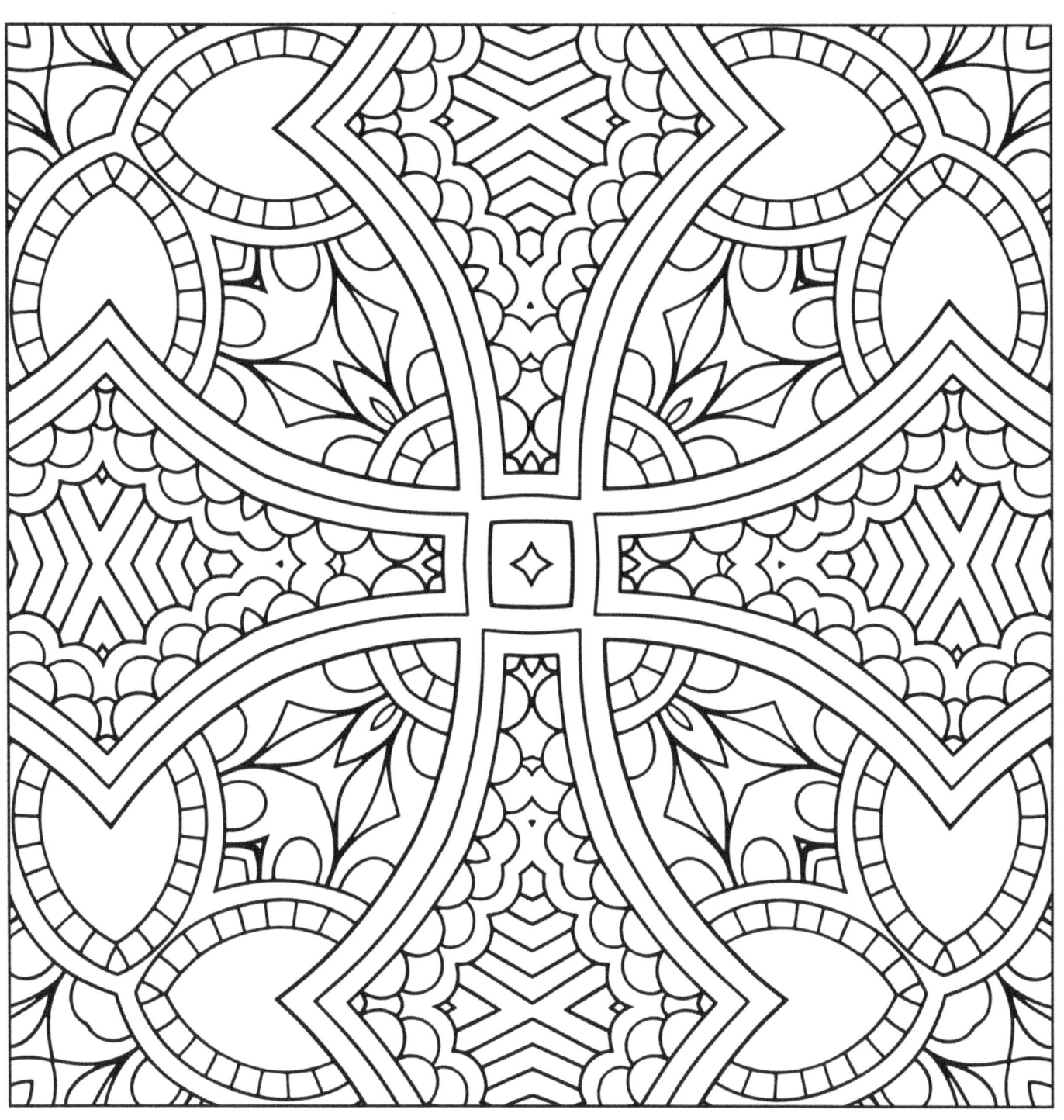

Laugh as much as you breathe and
love as long as you live.
~ Johnny Depp

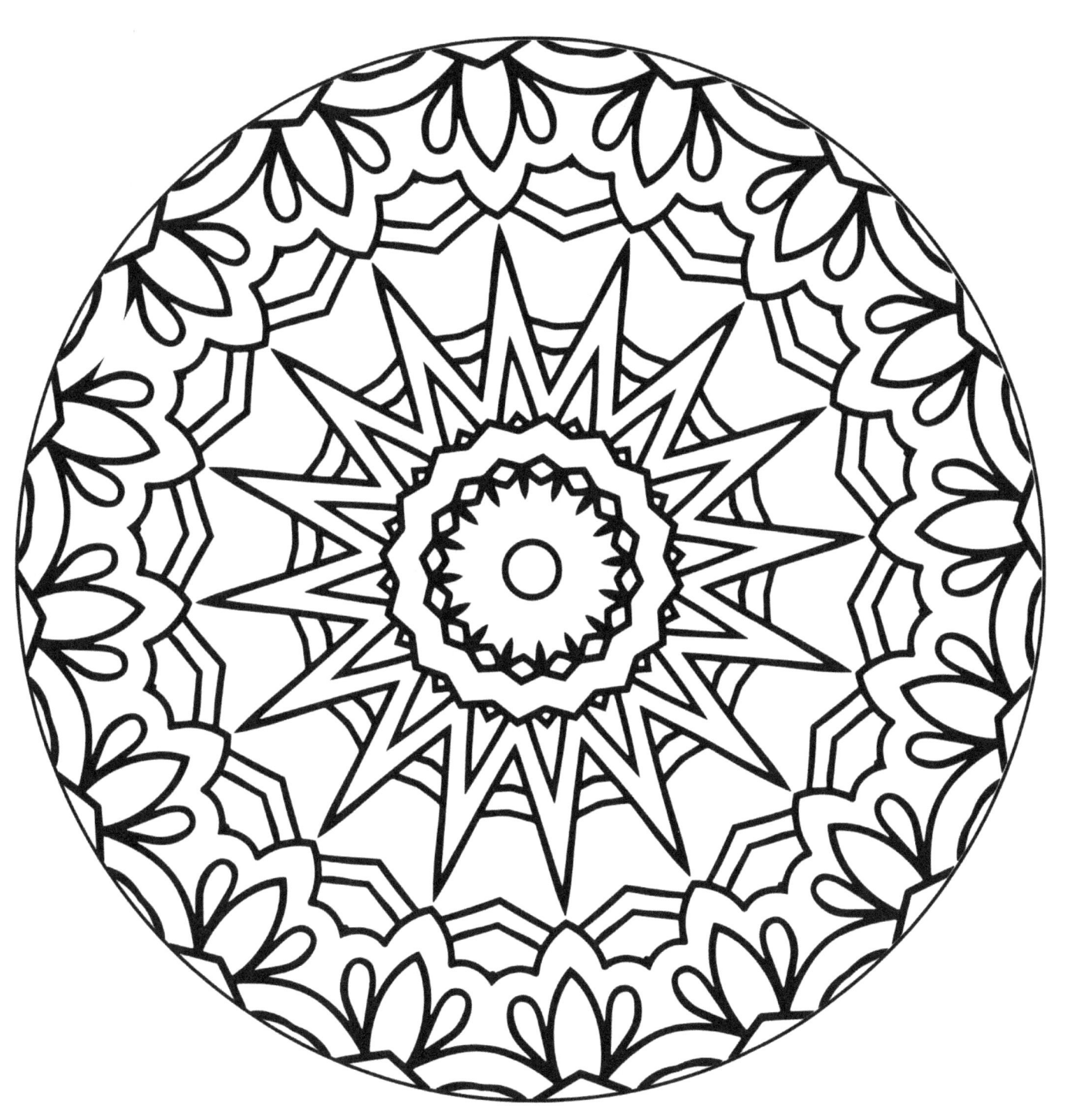

Faith is taking the first step when you don't see the whole stair case.

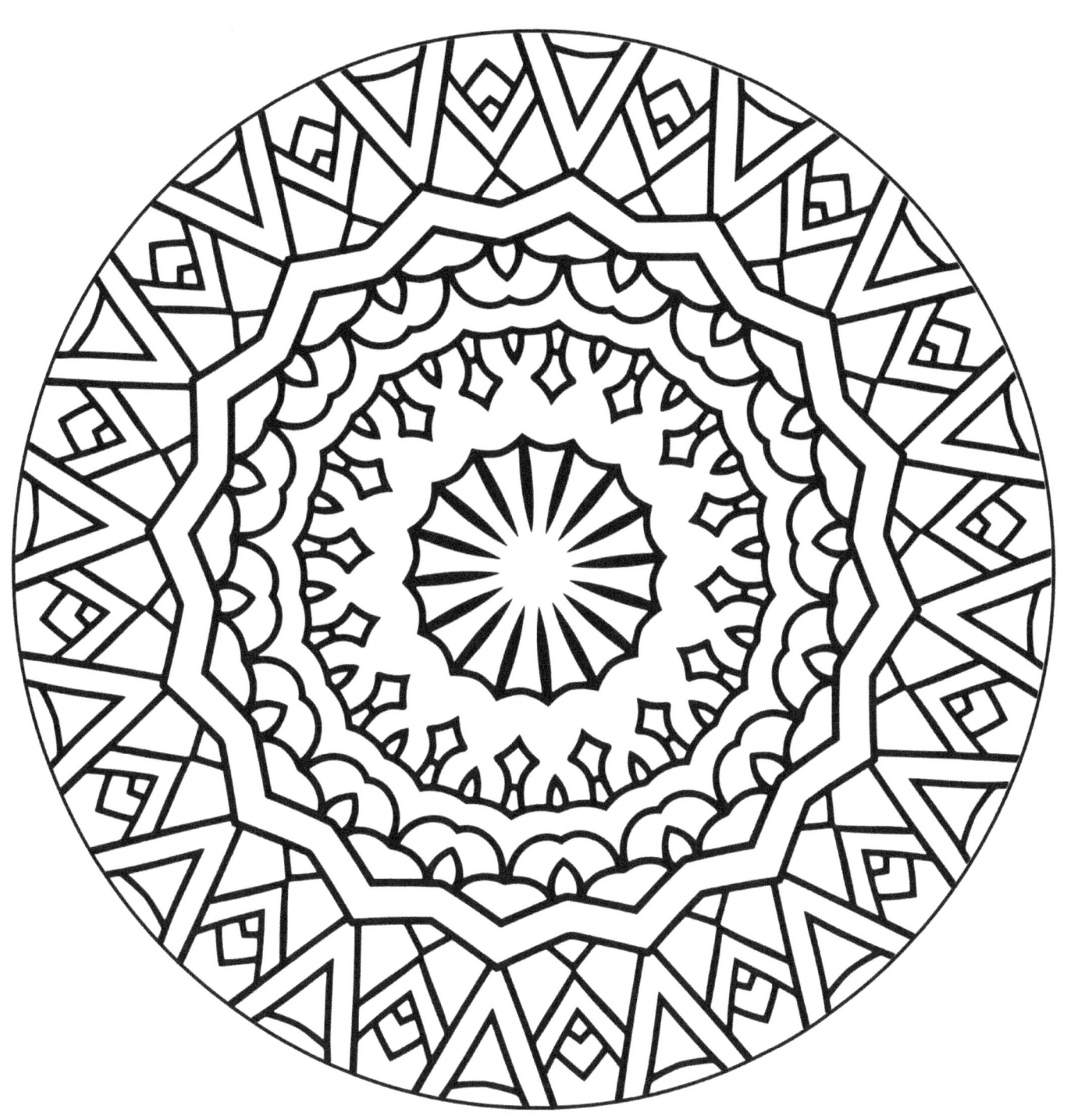

Only in the darkness can you see the stars. ~ Martin Luther King Jr.

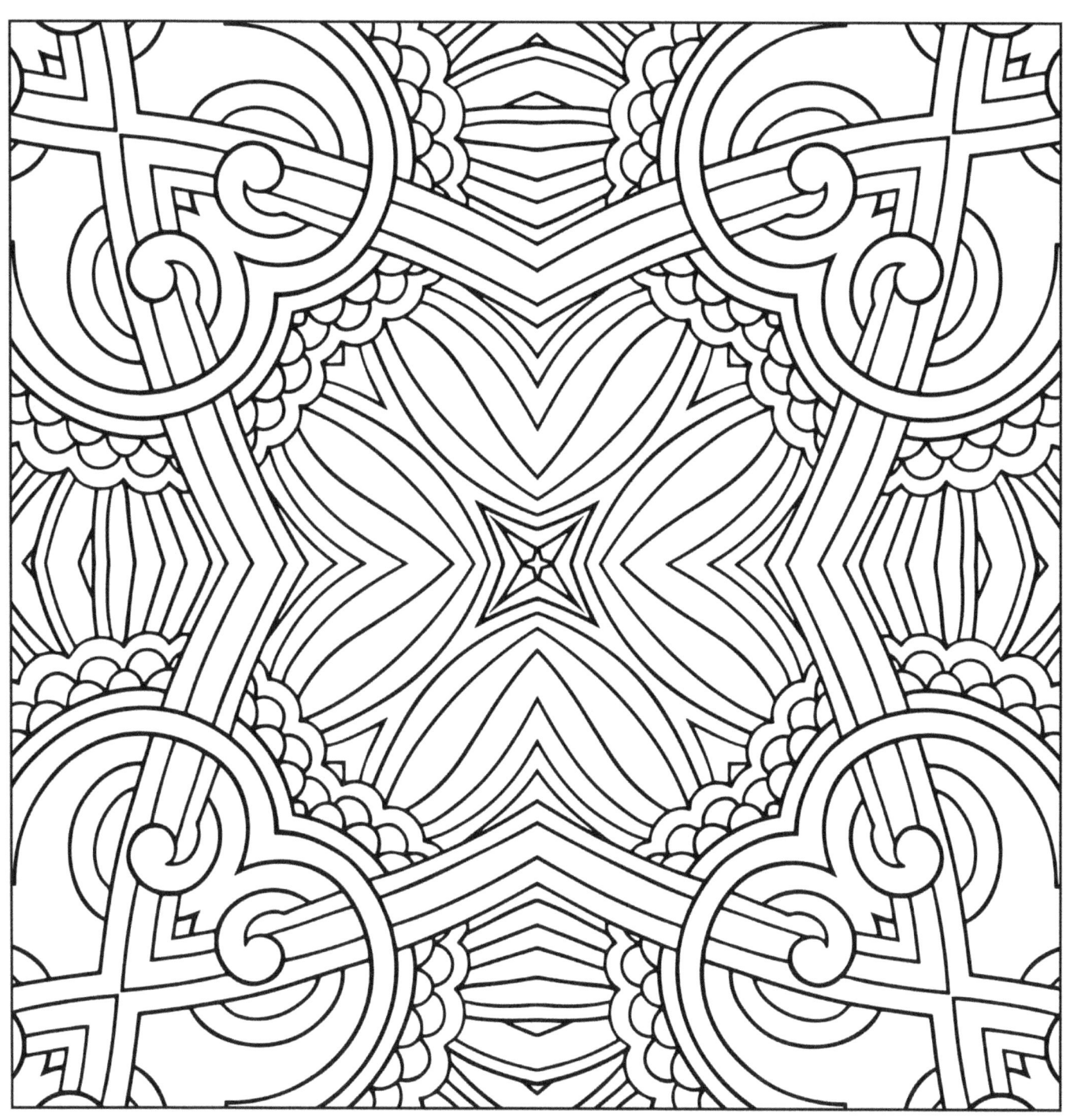

A flower does not think of competing to the flower next to it. It just blooms.

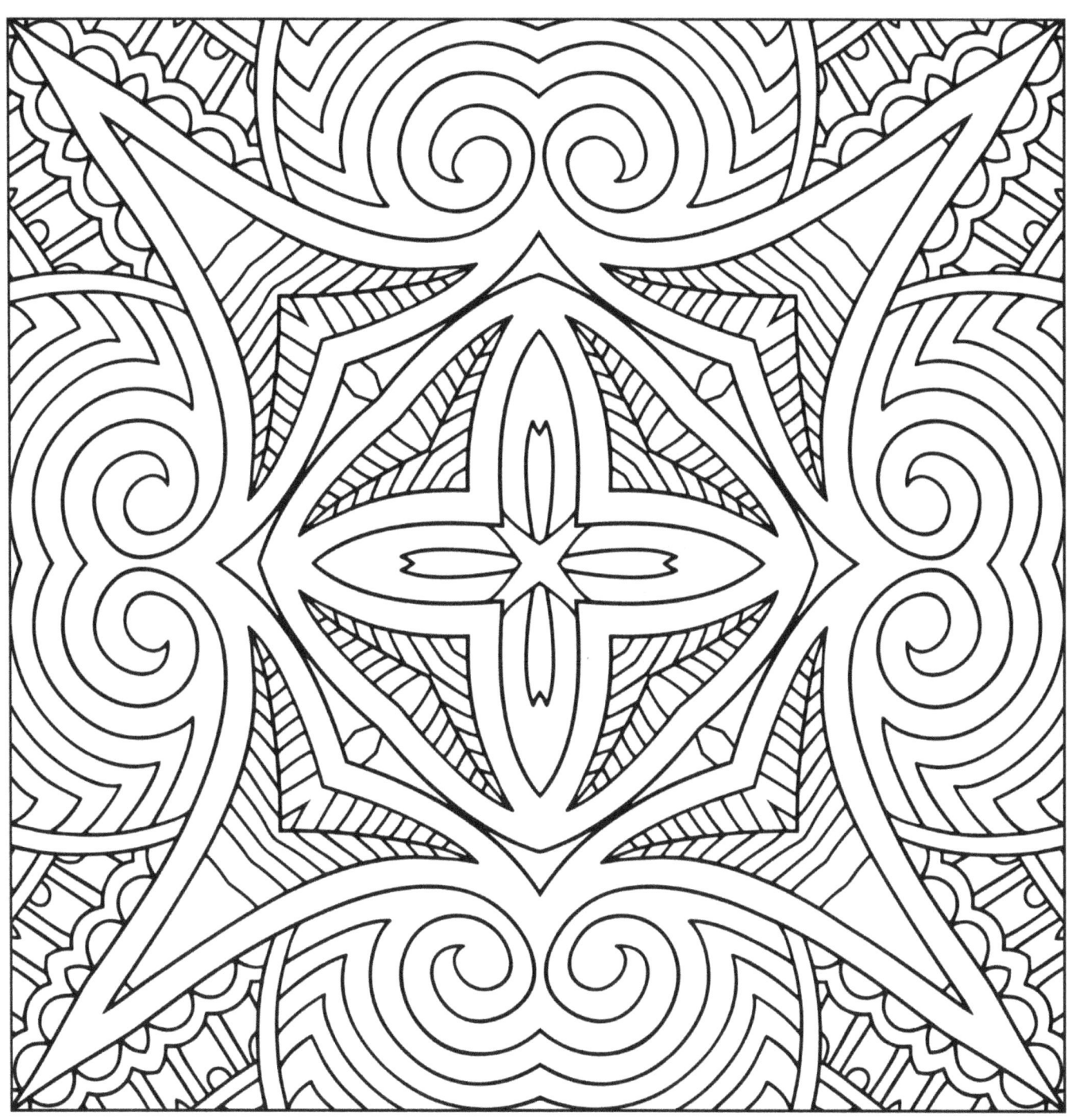

Smart has the plans, stupid has the stories.

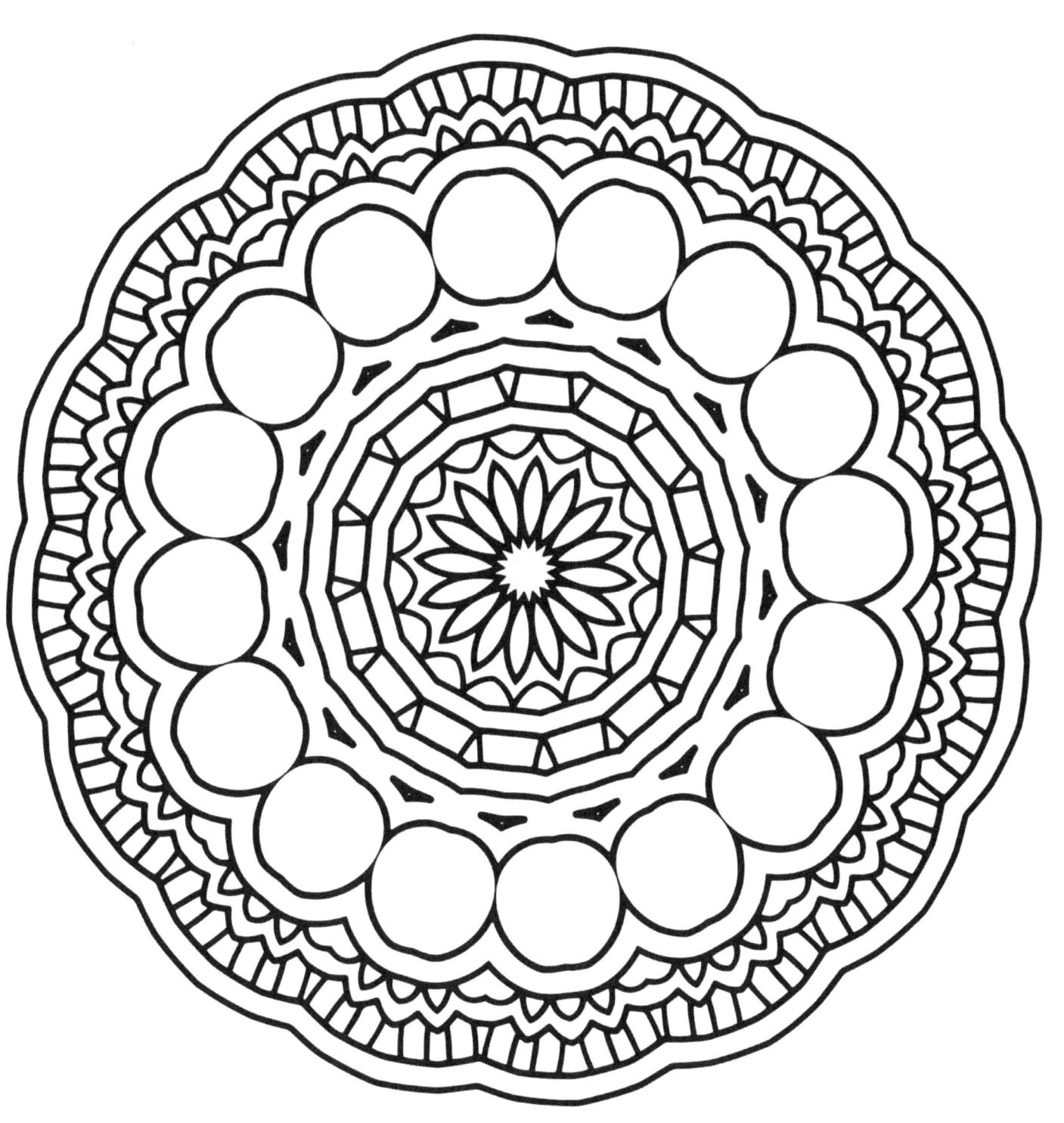

I like things to happen; and if they don't happen, I like to make them happen. ~ Martin Luther

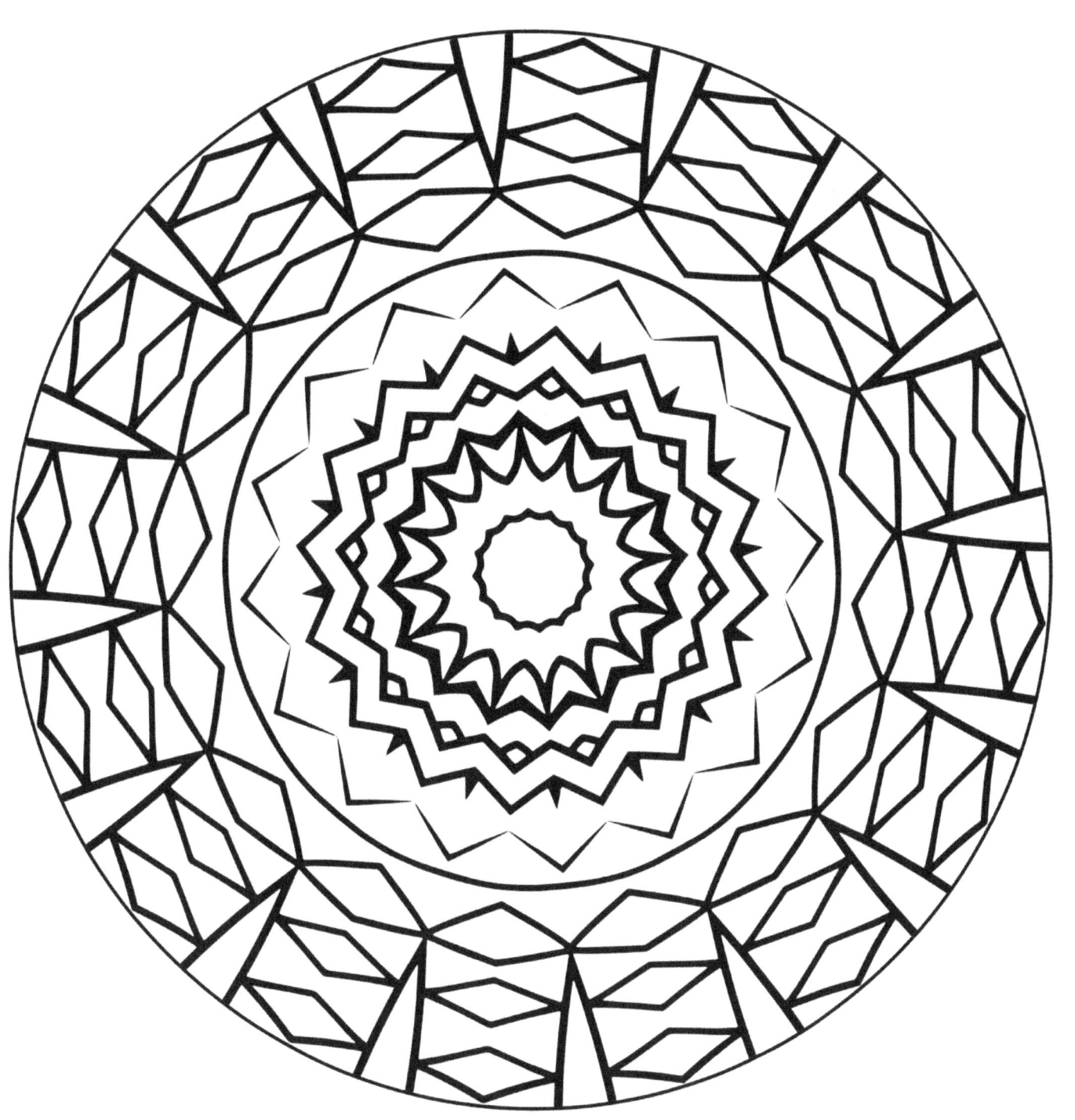

Raise your words not your voice. It is rain that grows flowers, not thunder. ~Rumi

Art is the most intense mode of individualism that the world has known. ~Oscar Wilde

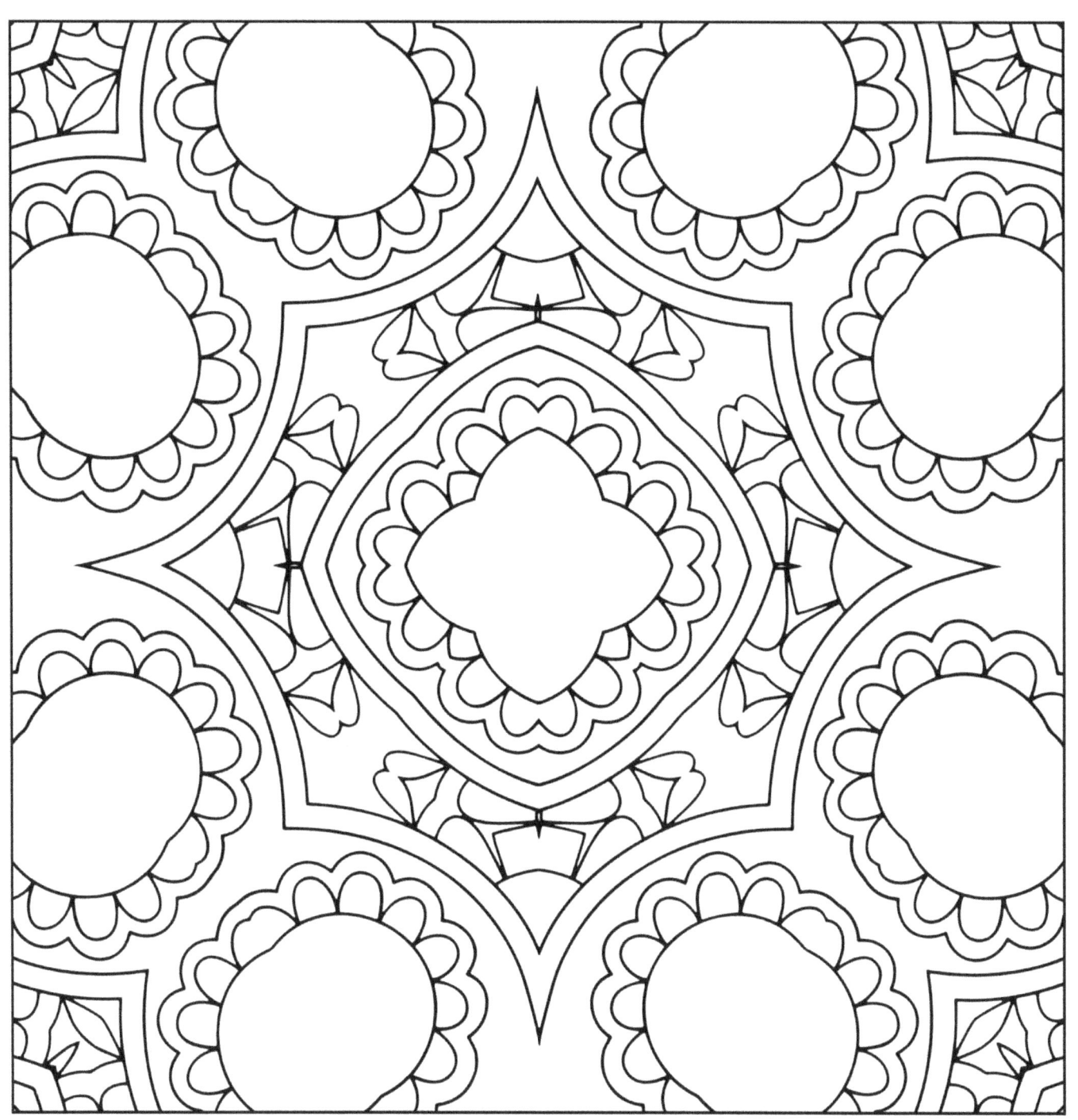

Thank you for coloring with me!

Look for more books in the future. If you have any feedback on this book I would love to hear it. Please send to
lovingtheoutdoors2013@gmail.com

Also enter my coloring contest for many prizes including a $100 Amazon Gift card, and having your picture displayed on the front of my next coloring book.

If you loved this book, please review it on Amazon.
Thank you.